The Ultimate Guide
DINOSAUR

Miles
KeLLy

First published in 2016 by
Miles Kelly Publishing Ltd

Harding's Barn, Bardfield End Green,
Thaxted, Essex, CM6 3PX, UK

Copyright © Miles Kelly Publishing Ltd 2016

2 4 6 8 10 9 7 5 3 1

Authors Rupert Matthews,
Steve Parker

Publishing Director Belinda Gallagher

Creative Director Jo Cowan

Editorial Director Rosie Neave

Cover Designer Simon Lee

Design Manager Simon Lee

Senior Designer Rob Hale

Image Manager Liberty Newton

Production Elizabeth Collins,
Caroline Kelly

Reprographics Stephan Davis,
Jennifer Cozens, Thom Allaway

ISBN 978-1-78209-990-1

Printed in China

British Library Cataloguing-in-Publication Data
A catalogue record for this book is available
from the British Library

Made with paper from a sustainable forest

www.mileskelly.net

ACKNOWLEDGEMENTS

Cover illustration Peter Bull Art Studio

All other artworks are from the Miles Kelly
Artwork Bank

The publishers would like to thank the following
sources for the use of their photographs:

Key: t = top, b = bottom, c = centre, l = left,
r = right, m = main

Acetate feature pages
Focus on T rex 16(t) Jerry LoFaro/Stocktrek
Images/Corbis; acetate (bl) MasPix/Alamy
Stock Photo, (c) Corbis; 17(l) Stocktrek Images,
Inc./Alamy Stock Photo, (r) Jim Young/Corbis,
(bl) Stocktrek Images, Inc./Alamy Stock Photo
Super sauropods 32(t) Jose Antonio Peñas/
Science Photo Library, 32(l) Roger Harris/
Science Photo Library, (b) Corey A. Ford/
Dreamstime.com; acetate (c) Patrick Dumas/
Look at Sciences/Science Photo Library,
(br) Natural History Museum, London/Science
Photo Library **Feeding and digestion**
40(l) Mark Stevenson/Stocktrek Images/
Corbis, (r) Louie Psihoyos/Corbis; acetate
(bl) Corbis **Eggs and nests** 48(t) Mohamad
Haghani/Stocktrek Images/Corbis; acetate
(t) Christian Darkin/Science Photo Library,
(br) Stocktrek Images, Inc./Alamy Stock
Photo; 49(bl) Catmando/Shutterstock.com,
(br) National Geographic Creative/Corbis
Fossil clues 56(cr) Steven Vidler/Corbis;
acetate (t) Claus Lunau/Science Photo Library,
(c) Dorling Kindersley/UIG/Science Photo
Library, (bl) The Natural History Museum/
Alamy Stock Photo; 57(bl) Bill Varie/Corbis
Fossil clues: 56(t) Louie Psihoyos, (tl) Scott
Smith, (bl) Louie Psihoyos, (cr) Steven Vidler;
57(bl) Bill Varie

Main pages
Alamy 26(b) MasPix; 36(b) Stocktrek Images,
Inc.
Corbis 6(t) Louie Psihoyos; 10(t) Mike
Hettwer/handout/dpa; 34(b) Roman Garcia
Mora/Stocktrek Images; 53(t) Louie Psihoyos;
55(b) Roman Garcia Mora/Stocktrek Images;
55(b) Roman Garcia Mora/Stocktrek Images;
59(t) Sergey Krasovskiy/Stocktrek Images,
(b) Colin Keates/Dorling Kindersley Ltd
Glow Images 28(b) Superstock
National Geographic Creative
53(b) Matthias Breiter/Minden Pictures;
61(b) Lowell Georgia
Rex Features 39(t) KPA/Zuma/REX/
Shutterstock
Science Photo Library 15(b) Jaime Chirinos;
22(b) Jaime Chirinos; 25(t) Jose Antonio Peñas;
28(t) Mark Hallett Paleoart; 42(b) Mark Hallett
Paleoart; 47 Laurie O'Keefe;
54(b) Natural History Museum, London
Shutterstock.com 8(b) Linda Bucklin;
9(t) John Kasawa; 11(t) Jean-Michel Girard;
13(b) Catmando; 18(t) Linda Bucklin;
18(b) Kostyantyn Ivanyshen; 21(b) Michael
Rosskothen; 21(t) Linda Bucklin; 22(t) Linda
Bucklin; 28(t) Linda Bucklin; 29(b) Catmando;
30(t) Catmando; 30(b) Michael Rosskothen;
34(t) Catmando; 35(t) Ralf Juergen Kraft;
44(b) Leonello Calvetti; 45(t) Leonello Calvetti;
46(b) ags1973; 47(t) DM7; 50(b) Ozja;
51(b) Leonello Calvetti; 62(b) Bob Orsillo

All other photographs are from: Corel,
digitalSTOCK, digitalvision, Fotolia,
iStock/Getty, PhotoDisc

Every effort has been made to acknowledge the
source and copyright holder of each picture.

Miles Kelly Publishing apologizes for any
unintentional errors or omissions.

Contents

THE DINOSAURS ARRIVE

MEAT-EATERS & RELATIVES

SAUROPODS & OTHER PLANT-EATERS

BIRD-HIPPED DINOSAURS

HOW THEY LIVED

WHERE IN THE WORLD

Age of Dinosaurs

● **The Age of Dinosaurs** refers to the time period called the Mesozoic Era, from about 252–66 mya (million years ago).

● **The Mesozoic Era** is divided into three shorter time spans – the Triassic, Jurassic and Cretaceous Periods.

● **In the Triassic Period**, 252–201 mya, dinosaurs began to evolve.

● **During the Jurassic Period** – about 201–145 mya – many dinosaurs reached their greatest size.

● **The Cretaceous Period** is when dinosaurs were at their most varied – about 145–66 mya.

● **All through the Mesozoic Era**, and before and since, the major landmasses gradually moved across the globe in a process known as continental drift.

● **In the Triassic Period**, all the continents were joined as one supercontinent – Pangaea.

● **In the Jurassic Period**, Pangaea separated into two huge landmasses – Laurasia in the north and Gondwana in the south.

● **In the Cretaceous Period**, Laurasia and Gondwana split, and the continents began to take the positions we know now.

● **The joining and separating** of the continents affected which kinds of dinosaurs lived where.

ERA	PERIOD	MYA
MESOZOIC	CRETACEOUS 145–66 MYA	70 80 90 100 110 120 130 140 150
	JURASSIC 201–145 MYA	160 170 180 190 200 210
	TRIASSIC 252–201 MYA	220 230 240 250

▲ *Dinosaurs ruled the land for 185 million years – longer than any other animal group.*

Archosaurs

● **Archosaurs were a large group** of reptiles that included the dinosaurs as one of their subgroups.

● **Other archosaur subgroups** included flying pterosaurs, crocodiles, and birds – since birds evolved from dinosaurs.

● **Pseudosuchians are living crocodilians** as were the lesser-known reptile group, the ornithosuchians, which were closely related to them but are now all extinct.

● **A dinosaur-like ornithosuchian** was *Ornithosuchus*, which gave its name to this group.

● **The 4-m-long** *Ornithosuchus* could stand almost upright and was probably a powerful predator.

● *Ornithosuchus* **fossils** have been found in Scotland.

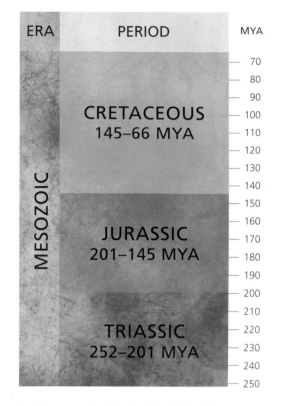

▶ *Ornithosuchus had a mix of features, both non-dinosaur (hips and back plates) and dinosaur (legs and skull).*

Ancestors

- **Experts have many opinions** about which group (or groups) of reptiles were the ancestors of the dinosaurs.

- **Very early dinosaurs** walked and ran on strong back limbs, so their ancestors probably did the same.

- **One group name** for dinosaurs' ancestors was the thecodonts, but this is no longer regarded as a true scientific grouping.

- **However there are several kinds** of small, slim, bipedal (walking on back legs), sharp-toothed reptiles that could show what dinosaur ancestors looked like.

- **Lagerperton**, 70 cm long, lived about 240 mya in Argentina, South America.

- **Marasuchus** was a similar creature but even smaller, less than 50 cm in length, also from Argentina.

- **Lagosuchus** was another small predator about 30 cm long from the same area, although it may have been the same as *Marasuchus*.

- **Euparkeria** from South Africa dates from 235 mya, but its rear legs were not as well developed.

◄ Euparkeria, or 'Parker's good animal', was named in 1913. It was about 60 cm in total length, slim and agile, and resembled the creatures from which dinosaurs probably evolved.

DID YOU KNOW?
The earliest known dinosaurs are from South America, so their ancestors probably came from here too.

Inventing the dinosaur

- **When fossils of dinosaurs** were first studied by scientists in the 1820s, they were thought to be from huge lizards, rhinoceroses or even whales.

▼ Megalosaurus was the first dinosaur to be given an official scientific name, even though the term 'dinosaur' had not yet been invented.

DID YOU KNOW?
The three main dinosaurs of the newly named Dinosauria in the 1840s were Iguanodon, Megalosaurus and Hylaeosaurus.

- **The first dinosaur** to be officially named in 1824 was *Megalosaurus*, by Englishman William Buckland.

- **Fossils of dinosaurs** were found and studied in 1822 by Gideon Mantell, a doctor in Sussex, southern England.

- **In 1825**, Mantell named the creature *Iguanodon*, because its teeth were very similar in shape to, but larger than, the teeth of the iguana lizard.

- **In the late 1830s**, British scientist Richard Owen realized that some fossils did not belong to lizards, but to an as yet unnamed group of reptiles.

- **In 1841–42**, Richard Owen invented a new name for the group of giant prehistoric reptiles – Dinosauria.

- **The name 'dinosaur'** means 'terrible lizard/reptile'.

- **Life-sized models** of several dinosaurs were made by British sculptor Waterhouse Hawkins in 1852–54.

- **Hawkins' models** were displayed at the Crystal Palace Exhibition in London, and caused a public sensation.

The importance of fossils

● **Most of the information** we know, or guess, about dinosaurs and other ancient life comes from fossils.

● **Fossils are the remains** of once-living things that have been preserved in rocks and turned to stone, usually over millions of years.

● **Many kinds of living things** from prehistoric times have left fossils, including mammals, birds, lizards, fish, and insects as well as plants, such as ferns and trees.

● **Modern methods** for fossil-hunting are powerful and accurate. Ground-penetrating radar, X-rays and computerized tomography can 'see' inside rock.

● **The dinosaur** *Oviraptor*, or 'egg thief', was named because one of its fossils suggested it was stealing the eggs of another dinosaur. X-rays actually revealed baby *Oviraptor*s inside the eggs. The 'egg thief' was probably guarding its own eggs when it died.

● **Fossils are big business**. In 2008 a 7-m-long fossil of *Triceratops* went on sale for £400,000.

● **Some fossils** are so rare, delicate or valuable that they are not put on display. Copies of rare fossils are sent to museums so that more people can study them.

● **Information about dinosaurs** comes not only from fossils of their body parts, but also from 'trace' fossils. These were not actual parts of their bodies, but other signs of their presence.

● **Trace fossils** include egg shells, footprints, claw and teeth marks, and coprolites – fossilized droppings.

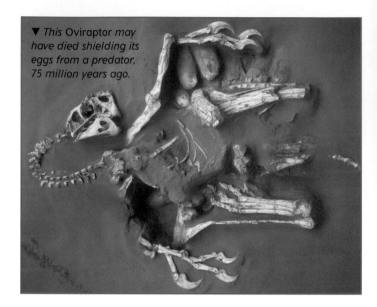

▼ *This* Oviraptor *may have died shielding its eggs from a predator, 75 million years ago.*

Fossil hunters

● **Many dinosaur fossils** were found in the USA in the 1870s–90s by Othniel Charles Marsh and Edward Drinker Cope.

● **Between 1877 and 1897**, Cope and Marsh found and described about 130 new kinds of dinosaurs.

● **Joseph Tyrrell** discovered fossils of *Albertosaurus* in 1884, in what became a very famous dinosaur region, the Red Deer River area of Alberta, Canada.

● **Lawrence Lambe** found many North American dinosaur fossils, such as *Centrosaurus* in 1904.

● **German fossil experts** Werner Janensch and Edwin Hennig led expeditions to east Africa in 1908–12, and discovered *Giraffatitan* and *Kentrosaurus*.

● **From 1933**, Yang Zhong-jiang (also called CC Young) led many fossil-hunting expeditions in China.

● **José Bonaparte** from Argentina has found many fossils in that region, including *Carnotaurus* in 1985.

● **Paul Sereno** from the University of Chicago has discovered and named huge dinosaurs and crocodiles from South America and North Africa.

▼ *Othniel Charles Marsh and Edward Drinker Cope had a rivalry between them that came to be known as the 'Bone Wars'. Allegedly, this began when Marsh pointed out a mistake that Cope had made with the reconstruction of a plesiosaur skeleton. Cope never forgave him, but the rift led to the discovery of almost 140 new dinosaur species.*

Edward Drinker Cope (1840–97)

Othniel Charles Marsh (1831–99)

Dinosaur names

- **Every dinosaur** has a scientific name, usually made up from Latin or Greek, place names or people's names, and written in *italics*.

- **Many dinosaur names** end in -*saurus*, which some scientists say means 'reptile' and others say means 'lizard' – but dinosaurs were not lizards.

- **Names often refer** to a unique feature a dinosaur had. *Baryonyx*, for example, means 'heavy claw', from the massive claw on its thumb.

- **Many dinosaur names** are real tongue-twisters, such as *Opisthocoelicaudia*, pronounced 'owe-pis-thowe-see-lee-cord-ee-ah'. The name means 'posterior tail cavity', and refers to the joints between the backbones in the dinosaur's tail.

- **Some dinosaurs** are named after the place where their fossils were found. *Minmi* was found near Minmi Crossing, Queensland, Australia.

◄ *The first fossil find of* Baryonyx *was its huge thumb claw.*

- **The fast-running ostrich dinosaurs** are named ornithomimosaurs, which means 'bird-mimic reptiles'.

- **More than 150 types** of dinosaur have been named after the people who first discovered their fossils, dug them up, or reconstructed the dinosaur.

- **The large duckbill (hadrosaur)** *Lambeosaurus* was named after Canadian fossil expert Lawrence Lambe.

- **Lambe worked mainly** during the early 1900s, and named one of his finds *Stephanosaurus*.

- **During the 1920s**, *Stephanosaurus* was renamed, along with *Didanodon*, as *Lambeosaurus*, in honour of Lambe's work.

- **The 4-m-long plant-eater** *Othnielia* was named after 19th-century fossil hunter Othniel Charles Marsh.

- ***Parksosaurus***, a 2.5-m-long plant-eater, was named in honour of Canadian dinosaur expert William Parks.

- **The full name** of the 'heavy claw' meat-eater *Baryonyx* is *Baryonyx walkeri*, after Bill Walker, the discoverer of its massive claw.

- **Part-time fossil hunter** Bill Walker found the claw in a clay pit quarry in Surrey, England.

◄ Alectrosaurus *means 'lonely lizard'. It lived 80–75 mya in Central Asia.*

The dinosaur orders

● **All dinosaurs are classified** in one of two large groups, according to the design and the shape of their hip bones.

● **One of these groups** is the Saurischia, meaning 'reptile-hipped'.

● **In a saurischian dinosaur**, the pubis bones (the lower front pair of rod-shaped bones in the pelvis) project down and forwards.

● **Almost all meat-eating dinosaurs** belonged to the Saurischia.

● **The biggest dinosaurs**, the plant-eating sauropods, also belonged to the Saurischia.

● **The second group** is the Ornithischia, meaning 'bird-hipped'.

● **In an ornithischian dinosaur**, the pubis bones project down and backwards, lying parallel with another pair, the ischium bones.

● **All dinosaurs** in the Ornithischia group, from small *Heterodontosaurus* to huge *Triceratops*, were plant-eaters.

◄ *In the Ornithischia or 'bird hips', the pubis angles down and backwards.*

Ilium

Ilium

▶ *In the Saurischia or 'lizard hips', the projecting strut of the hip bone, known as the pubis, is angled down and forwards.*

Pubis

Ischium

Ischium

Pubis

DID YOU KNOW?

The classifying of dinosaurs according to their hip structure goes back to 1888.

Legs and posture

● **All dinosaurs had four limbs**. Unlike some other reptiles, such as snakes and slow-worms, they did not lose their limbs through evolution.

● **Some dinosaurs**, such as the massive, plant-eating sauropod *Janenschia*, stood and walked on all four legs nearly all the time.

● **The all-fours method** of standing and walking is called quadrupedal.

● **Some dinosaurs**, such as the nimble, meat-eating dromaeosaur *Deinonychus*, stood and walked on their back limbs only.

● **The back-limbs-only method** of standing and walking is called bipedal.

● **Some dinosaurs**, such as the hadrosaur *Edmontosaurus*, could move on all four limbs or just on their back legs if they chose to.

● **The two- or four-legs method** of standing and walking is called bipedal/quadrupedal.

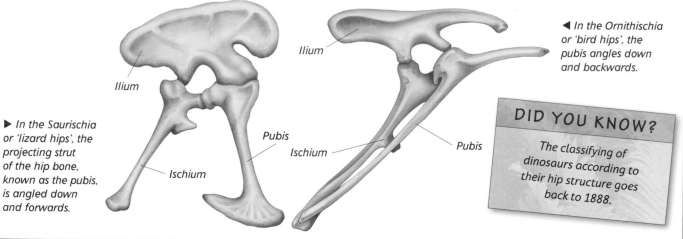

▲ Brachiosaurus *had the typical quadrupedal posture, using all four legs.*

▲ Tarbosaurus, *an Asian type of Tyrannosaurus, was a bipedal dinosaur that ran and walked on its strong back legs. These contrasted hugely to its puny front arms, which were too small to be used.*

● **Reptiles such as lizards** and crocodiles have a sprawling posture, in which the upper legs join the body at the sides.

● **Dinosaurs had an upright posture**, with the legs directly below the body.

● **The more efficient upright posture** and gait may be one major reason why dinosaurs were so successful compared to other animals of the time.

Warm or cold blood?

- **If dinosaurs were cold-blooded**, like reptiles today, they would have been slow or inactive in cold conditions.

- **If dinosaurs were warm-blooded**, like birds and mammals today, they would have been able to stay warm and active in cold conditions.

- **Experts once believed** that all dinosaurs were cold-blooded, but today there is much disagreement.

- **Some evidence** for warm-bloodedness comes from the structure of fossil bones.

- **The structure** of some dinosaur bones is more like that of warm-blooded creatures than of reptiles.

- **Some small meat-eating dinosaurs** very probably evolved into birds. As birds are warm-blooded, these dinosaurs may have been warm-blooded too.

- **If some dinosaurs were warm-blooded**, they would probably have needed to eat at least ten times more food than if they were cold-blooded, to 'burn' food energy to make heat.

- **In a 'snapshot' count** of dinosaur fossils, the number of predators compared to prey is more like the comparisons seen in mammals than in reptiles.

- **Many small meat-eaters** are now known to have had feathers. One reason could be as insulation, to keep in body heat if the dinosaur was warm-blooded.

◄ *Crocodiles, which were around even in the very earliest dinosaur period (the Triassic) are cold-blooded.*

Early dinosaurs

- **The first dinosaurs** had appeared about 230 mya, in the Middle Triassic Period.

- **These dinosaurs** were small-to-medium meat-eaters with sharp teeth and claws. They ran quickly on their two longer, stronger back legs.

- **Fossils of *Herrerasaurus*** date from 230 mya and were found near San Juan in Argentina, South America.

- ***Herrerasaurus* was about** 3–5 m in total length, and probably weighed some 200–250 kg.

- **Perhaps slightly earlier**, about 231 mya, and in the same place as *Herrerasaurus*, there lived a similar-shaped dinosaur named *Eoraptor*, which was only 1–1.5 m long and weighed 10 kg.

- **The name *Eoraptor*** means 'dawn plunderer' or 'early thief'.

- ***Staurikosaurus*** was a meat-eater similar to *Herrerasaurus*. It is known to have lived around 225 mya, in present-day Brazil, South America.

- ***Procompsognathus* was another** early meat-eater. It lived 210 mya in the Late Triassic Period in Germany.

- ***Pisanosaurus* lived in Argentina** in the Late Triassic Period, and was only one metre long. It may have been a plant-eater.

▲ *The very early meat-eater Herrerasaurus dates to about 230 mya.*

DID YOU KNOW?

Eoraptor *and* Herrerasaurus *hunted small animals such as lizards, insects and lizard-like reptiles.*

Eodromaeus

- *Eodromaeus* **was one** of several small, bipedal (walking on two legs) dinosaurs from early in their time.

- **Its fossils were discovered** in Argentina in 1996, and at first they were thought to be from the similar *Eoraptor*.

- **More studies showed** they were a different dinosaur, which was named *Eodromaeus*, meaning 'dawn runner', in 2011.

- *Eodromaeus* **lived** about 230 mya during the early part of the Late Triassic Period, making it one of the earliest known dinosaurs.

- **It was quite small**, with a nose–tail length of 1.2 m. It was slim too, weighing 4–6 kg.

- **Its rear legs were much larger**, longer and stronger than the front ones, which were more like arms.

- **This body build indicates** a fast, nimble creature that could dart and zigzag away from bigger predators.

- **The top speed of** *Eodromaeus* is estimated at anywhere between 25 and 40 km/h.

▲ *The skull of* Eodromaeus *has widely gaping jaws, with the jaw joint at the rear, and small sharp teeth suited to eating bugs and worms.*

DID YOU KNOW?

Eodromaeus and other fossils were found in Ischigualasto Park's Valle de la Luna, 'Valley of the Moon', named from its strange, stark rock formations.

- **Like** *Eoraptor*, *Eodromaeus* probably snapped up small bugs, worms and little reptiles.

Coelophysis

- *Coelophysis* **was a small, agile dinosaur** that lived early in the Age of Dinosaurs, about 220–200 mya.

- **A huge collection** of *Coelophysis* fossils was discovered in the 1940s, at a place called Ghost Ranch, New Mexico, USA.

- **Hundreds of** *Coelophysis* were preserved together at Ghost Ranch – possibly a herd that drowned in a flood.

- *Coelophysis* **was almost 3 m** in total length. Its slim, lightweight build meant that it probably weighed only 15–25 kg.

- *Coelophysis* **belonged** to the group of mostly meat-eating dinosaurs known as theropods. It probably ate small animals such as insects, worms and lizards.

- **Long, powerful back legs** allowed *Coelophysis* to run fast.

- **The front limbs** were like arms, each with a hand bearing three large, strong, sharp-clawed fingers to grab prey, and one small, non-functional finger.

- **The bird-like skull** was filled with small, sharp teeth.

- *Coelophysis* **means** 'hollow form'. It was so-named because some of its bones were hollow, like the bones of birds, making it lightly built.

◀ Coelophysis *would have stood almost waist-high to a person as it darted about on its long back legs.*

Dilophosaurus

● **Dilophosaurus was** a large meat-eating theropod dinosaur that lived about 195–190 mya.

● **Fossils of Dilophosaurus** were found in Arizona, USA, and possibly other parts of the USA.

▼ Dilophosaurus *is one of the first big, powerful, predatory dinosaurs known from fossil evidence.*

● **The crests** were too thin and fragile to be used for head-butting.

● **Brightly coloured skin** may have covered the crests, as a visual display to rivals or enemies.

● **The fossils in Arizona** were discovered by Jesse Williams, a Navajo Native American, in 1942.

● **Studying the fossils** proved very difficult, and the dinosaur was not given its official name until 1970.

● **Dilophosaurus measured** about 6–7 m from its nose to the end of its very long tail.

● **The name Dilophosaurus** means 'two-ridged reptile', from the two thin, rounded, bony crests on its head, each shaped like half a dinner plate.

DID YOU KNOW?

Dilophosaurus *probably weighed over 500 kg – as heavy as the biggest polar bears today.*

Eustreptospondylus

DID YOU KNOW?

Eustreptospondylus *means 'well-curved backbone'. This is due to the arrangement of its spine as seen in fossils.*

● **Eustreptospondylus was a large meat-eater** that lived in present-day Oxfordshire and Buckinghamshire, in England. It lived about 165–160 mya.

● **In the 1870s**, a fairly complete skeleton of a young *Eustreptospondylus* was found near Oxford, but was named as *Megalosaurus*, the only other big meat-eater known from the region.

● **In 1964**, British fossil expert Alick Walker showed that the Oxford dinosaur was not *Megalosaurus*, and gave it a new name, *Eustreptospondylus*.

● **A full-grown Eustreptospondylus** measured about 6 m in length and is estimated to have weighed over 400 kg, although the Oxford specimen was only part-grown.

● **In its enormous mouth**, *Eustreptospondylus* had a great number of small, sharp teeth.

● **Eustreptospondylus** may have hunted sauropods such as *Cetiosaurus* and stegosaurs, two groups of dinosaurs that roamed the region at the time.

▲ *The fossils of* Eustreptospondylus *were found with those of sea creatures, suggesting it may have hunted along the seashore. This medium-sized theropod weighed about the same as two very large lions.*

Sciurimimus

- **The name *Sciurimimus*** means 'squirrel mimic' and was given to this dinosaur in 2012.

- **The name comes from the tail** of this dinosaur, which has filament-like or fibre-like feathers along its length – reminiscent of a squirrel's bushy tail.

- **Only one fossil of *Sciurimimus*** is known to date, from Bavaria, southwest Southern Germany.

- **The fossil is in fine-grained limestone** dated to the Late Jurassic Period, some 150 mya.

- **The fossilized remains** are very detailed, showing up fine features such as the tail feathers.

- **Details of the bones** show that this specimen of *Sciurimimus* was a juvenile, not yet fully grown.

- **The nose–tail length** of the *Sciurimimus* fossil is 70 cm, but the dinosaur could have been over one metre long when adult.

- ***Sciurimimus* had small sharp teeth** and probably preyed on small creatures such as insects.

- **Although *Sciurimimus* had feathers**, it was not related to the main groups of bird-like feathered dinosaurs – showing that feather-like coverings evolved in widely separate kinds of dinosaurs.

◄ *The fast-moving, agile dinosaur* Sciurimimus *lived at about the same time, and in the same region, as the early bird* Archaeopteryx.

Baryonyx

- ***Baryonyx*** was a large meat-eating dinosaur that lived about 130 mya.

- **The first fossil find** of *Baryonyx* was its huge thumb claw, discovered in Surrey, England, in 1983.

- **The total length** of *Baryonyx* was 9–10 m.

- ***Baryonyx* had a slim build** and a long, narrow tail, and probably weighed less than 2 tonnes.

- **The snout was unusual** for a meat-eating dinosaur because it was very long and narrow – similar to today's slim-snouted crocodiles.

- **The teeth were long** and slim, especially at the front of the mouth.

- **The general similarities** between *Baryonyx* and a crocodile suggest that *Baryonyx* may have been a fish-eater.

- **It may have lurked** in swamps or close to rivers, darting its head forward on its long, flexible neck to snatch fish.

- **The massive thumb claw**, which measured 35 cm in length, may have been used to hook fish or amphibians from the water.

- **The dinosaur was named** after this outsized feature – the name *Baryonyx* means 'heavy claw'.

▲ *Fossils of* Baryonyx *were found with fish scales, suggesting it was a semi aquatic fish-catcher.*

DID YOU KNOW?

The fossil skeleton of Baryonyx was over two thirds complete, allowing experts to learn many details of its lifestyle.

Allosaurus

- **A big meat-eater**, *Allosaurus* was almost the same size as *Tyrannosaurus*. It lived about 155–150 mya, during the Late Jurassic Period.

- *Allosaurus* **was up to 11–12 m** in total length and its weight is variously estimated between 1.5 and 4 tonnes.

- **The head** was almost one metre in length, but its skull was light, with large gaps, or 'windows', that would have been covered by muscle and skin.

- **Not only could** *Allosaurus* open its jaws in a huge gape, it could also flex them so that the whole mouth became wider, for an even bigger bite.

- **Most** *Allosaurus* **fossils** come from the states in the American Midwest, especially Utah, Colorado and Wyoming.

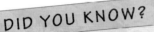

DID YOU KNOW?

The remains of 60 Allosaurus were found in the Cleveland-Lloyd Dinosaur Quarry, Utah, USA.

- *Allosaurus* **may have hunted** giant sauropod dinosaurs such as *Diplodocus*, *Camarasaurus* and *Brachiosaurus*.

- **Fossils similar to** *Allosaurus* were identified in Europe and Africa, and a smaller 'dwarf' version was found in Australia.

▼ Allosaurus *almost rivalled* Tyrannosaurus *in size, but lived 90 million years earlier.*

Carnotaurus

- **The big, powerful, meat-eating** *Carnotaurus* belongs to the theropod dinosaur group. It lived about 75–70 mya.

- *Carnotaurus* **fossils** come mainly from the Chubut region of Argentina, South America.

- **A medium-sized dinosaur,** *Carnotaurus* was about 8–9 m in total length and weighed more than one tonne.

- **The skull was relatively tall** from top to bottom and short from front to back, compared to other meat-eaters such as *Allosaurus* and *Tyrannosaurus*. This gave *Carnotaurus* a snub-snouted appearance.

- **The name** *Carnotaurus* means 'meat-eating bull', referring partly to its bull-like face.

- *Carnotaurus* had two cone-shaped bony crests, or 'horns', one above each eye.

- **Rows of extra-large scales**, like small lumps, ran along *Carnotaurus* from head to tail.

◀ *The first, and so far only, fossil remains of* Carnotaurus *were discovered in 1984 and the dinosaur was named in 1985. It had small pebble-like scales embedded in its skin.*

- **Like** *Tyrannosaurus*, *Carnotaurus* had small front limbs that could not reach its mouth and may have had no use.

- *Carnotaurus* **probably ate** plant-eating dinosaurs such as *Chubutisaurus*, although its teeth and jaws were not especially big or strong.

Yutyrannus

● **Named in 2012**, *Yutyrannus* or 'feathered tyrant' is a large predator dinosaur in the same group as the great *Tyrannosaurus*.

● **However, it lived** almost 60 million years earlier than *Tyrannosaurus*, about 125 mya, in what is now northwest China.

● *Yutyrannus* **was almost 9 m long** and could have weighed more than 1.5 tonnes.

● **It is the biggest dinosaur** so far that has feathers preserved with its fossil bones and teeth.

● **The feathers were slim**, flexible filaments, some more than 15 cm long.

● **Different specimens** of *Yutyrannus* have feathers on different parts of the body, so taking them all together, the filaments could have covered most of the dinosaur.

● **The skull of the largest** *Yutyrannus* specimen is almost one metre long.

● **It also had a small 'horn'** above each eye, like several other tyrannosaur-group dinosaurs.

● **Like its relatives**, *Yutyrannus* was a powerful predator with a huge mouth and many sharp teeth.

▲ Yutyrannus *lived in a region that was quite cool 125 mya, so its hair-like or plume-like feathers may have helped to control its body temperature.*

Tyrannosaurus

● *Tyrannosaurus, or T rex*, is one of the most famous dinosaurs. Several discoveries have revealed fossilized bones, teeth and entire skeletons.

● *T rex* **lived** about 68–66 mya. It was 12 m long and weighed 7 tonnes.

● **Its full name** is *Tyrannosaurus rex*, which means 'king of the tyrant reptiles'.

● **The head** was 1.2 m long and had more than 50 dagger-like teeth, some longer than 15 cm.

● *T rex* **fossils** have been found at many sites in North America including Alberta and Saskatchewan in Canada, and Colorado, Wyoming, Montana and New Mexico in the USA.

● **The arms and hands** of *T rex* were tiny, and may have had no use at all.

● **Recent fossil finds** of a group of *T rex* include youngsters, suggesting that they may have lived as families in small herds or packs.

● *T rex* **may have been** an active hunter, chasing after its fleeing prey, or it may have been a skulking scavenger that ambushed old and sickly victims.

DID YOU KNOW?

Until the 1990s, T rex was known as the biggest meat-eating animal ever. Its record was broken by Giganotosaurus and then Spinosaurus.

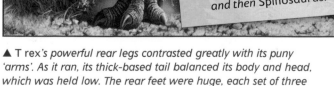

▲ T rex's *powerful rear legs contrasted greatly with its puny 'arms'. As it ran, its thick-based tail balanced its body and head, which was held low. The rear feet were huge, each set of three toes supporting some 3–4 tonnes.*

Carcharodontosaurus

- *Carcharodontosaurus* was one of the biggest meat-eating dinosaurs and land predators ever, rivalling *Tyrannosaurus* and similar types.

- **Some of its fossils** are very detailed, with the cavity inside the skull showing the shape of the dinosaur's brain, including the parts dealing with sight and smell.

- *Carcharodontosaurus'* teeth were about 20 cm long and triangular in shape.

- **The whole dinosaur** was about 13 m in total length and very powerfully built, with a weight of perhaps 10 tonnes.

- **Putting together** several specimen finds shows the skull was up to 1.7 m long.

- *Carcharodontosaurus* **lived** in North Africa about 100–95 mya, when the region had rivers, lakes, swamps and forests.

- **Its fossils** were first dug up in 1925, but more, larger specimens unearthed in the 1990s showed its true size.

▲ Carcharodontosaurus was not the largest predator of its time and place, since the even greater Spinosaurus roamed the same region some 100 mya.

DID YOU KNOW?

Carcharodontosaurus was named 'ragged tooth reptile' after the shark, Carcharodon carcharias, due to jagged serrations along its teeth.

- *Carcharodontosaurus* **belonged** to the group known as Carnosauria, which used to include all kinds of big meat-eaters but has recently been restricted to just a few kinds.

- **A cousin of** *Carcharodontosaurus* may have been *Allosaurus* from North America, which lived about 50 million years before and was almost as large.

Mapusaurus

- *Mapusaurus* **is in the top ten** of giant meat-eating dinosaurs.

- **Fossils from parts** of several individuals were excavated from 1997 at Cañadón del Gato, Neuquén Province, Argentina.

- **The rocks containing** *Mapusaurus* fossils are around 95 million years old.

- **More than 170 bones** and parts of bones have been recovered, from up to nine different individuals of different sizes.

- **The main fossils suggest** *Mapusaurus* was at least 10 m long, and clues from larger bone fragments could make the length 13 m and weight over 8 tonnes.

- *Mapusaurus* **was probably related** to another great predator, *Giganotosaurus*, from the same area and a similar time span.

- **Close inspection of the fossils** showed that some individuals had been injured, with their bones mending, while other bones revealed signs of infection.

- **The science of studying injuries** and diseases in prehistoric animals and plants is known as paleoepidemiology.

- **Finding remains** of so many individuals together could indicate *Mapusaurus*, whose name means 'earth lizard', lived and perhaps even hunted in groups.

▼ Mapusaurus *lived in a region that was generally dry, but with seasonal flood streams that probably attracted large prey to drink at waterholes.*

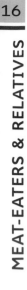

Focus on *T rex*

Tyrannosaurus rex, 'T Rex' for short, was one of the most powerful and dangerous meat-eating dinosaurs.
T rex lived in the western parts of North America between about 68–65 million years ago. Compared to other large meat-eaters, its fossils have been found over a wide area of land, indicating that it must have been a very successful animal.

It is thought that young *T rex* may have stayed in or near the nest for the first few weeks of life. The parents may have brought them food and protected them from other hunters.

The young dinosaurs probably fed on lizards, mammals and other small animals. By the time it was about 12 years old, *T rex* would have weighed around one tonne. Then there began a very rapid increase in size. Each year, *T rex* would have gained about 600 kg in weight until it was 18 years old and fully grown.

▶ *GROWING UP*
In its early years, T rex grew rapidly. This growth would have been fuelled by the consumption of massive amounts of meat.

▶ *HATCHING OUT*
When it hatched, a baby T rex may have weighed around 20 kg. It would have emerged with teeth and claws, ready to find its own food.

Because so many different fossils of *T rex* have been found we know a lot about its life cycle. Young *T rex* hatched from eggs. They may have been cared for by their parents for the first few months of life. For the next five years the young grew slowly. They probably hid in undergrowth where they would be safe from larger dinosaurs.

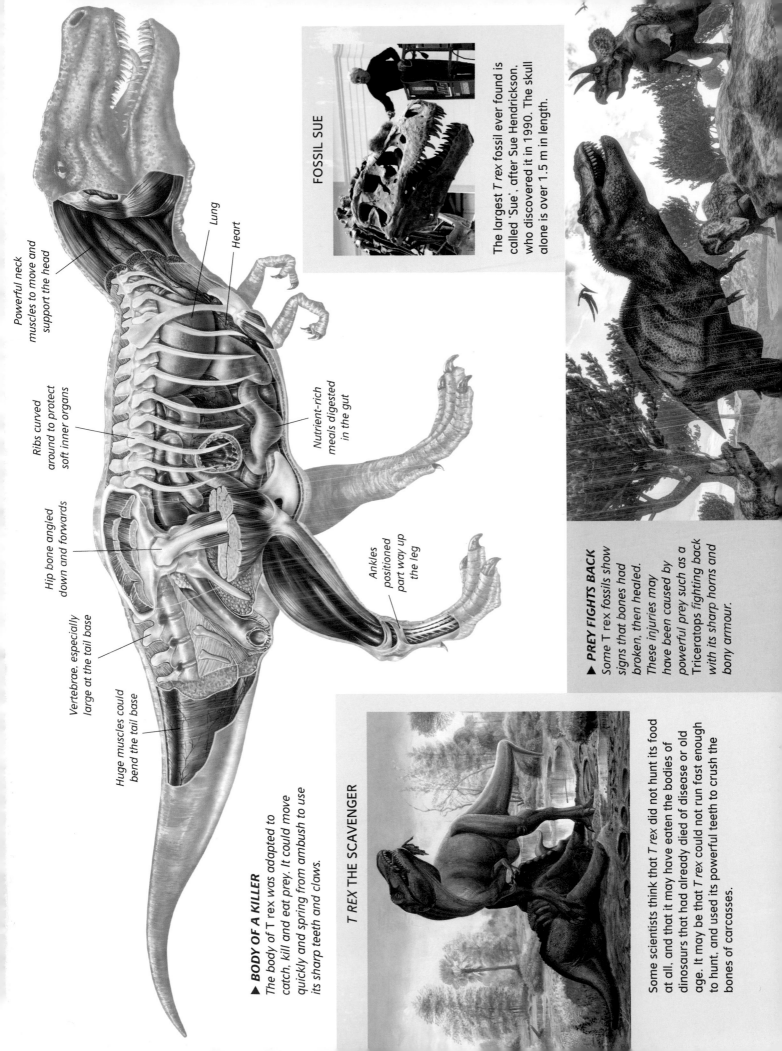

Powerful neck muscles to move and support the head

Lung

Heart

The largest T rex fossil ever found is called 'Sue', after Sue Hendrickson, who discovered it in 1990. The skull alone is over 1.5 m in length.

Ribs curved around to protect soft inner organs

Nutrient-rich meals digested in the gut

Hip bone angled down and forwards

Ankles positioned part way up the leg

Vertebrae, especially large at the tail base

Huge muscles could bend the tail base

▶ **PREY FIGHTS BACK**
Some T rex fossils show signs that bones had broken, then healed. These injuries may have been caused by powerful prey such as a Triceratops fighting back with its sharp horns and bony armour.

▶ **BODY OF A KILLER**
The body of T rex was adapted to catch, kill and eat prey. It could move quickly and spring from ambush to use its sharp teeth and claws.

T REX THE SCAVENGER

Some scientists think that T rex did not hunt its food at all, and that it may have eaten the bodies of dinosaurs that had already died of disease or old age. It may be that T rex could not run fast enough to hunt, and used its powerful teeth to crush the bones of carcasses.

Giganotosaurus

● **In 1994** there was great news that remains of a meat-eating dinosaur even bigger than *Tyrannosaurus* had been found in Patagonia, in the south of Argentina.

● **The new find** was named as *Giganotosaurus*, 'giant southern lizard'.

● **The length of *Giganotosaurus*** was estimated at up to 13 m, and the weight between 8 and 10 tonnes.

● **The skull** was at first said to be 1.8 m in length, although this was then reduced to 1.6 m. It is still one of the most massive skulls of any dinosaur.

● **The remains of *Giganotosaurus*** were first noticed by Rubén Carolini, a local vehicle mechanic who went fossil-hunting in his spare time.

● **Its full name is *Giganotosaurus carolinii***, in honour of its discoverer.

● **Carolini went on to become** Director of the Villa El Chocón Municipal Museum, which celebrates his enormous find.

● **The main *Giganotosaurus* find** was an exceptional specimen, almost three-quarters complete.

▲ Giganotosaurus *had three clawed fingers on each hand, and the hands and arms were not as undersized as those of* Tyrannosaurus.

● ***Giganotosaurus* lived** around 100–95 mya.

● **Not far away**, the fossils of the colossal plant-eater *Argentinosaurus* were located, which lived around the same time – perhaps a victim of *Giganotosaurus*?

Spinosaurus

● **No other meat-eating dinosaur**, or any other land-based carnivore, found so far is as big as *Spinosaurus*.

● **This immense predator** has been known for over 100 years, but new finds in the 1990s and 2000s show that it is the new record-holder.

● **The original *Spinosaurus* fossils** came from Egypt in 1912. They were named in 1915 by German palaeontologist Ernst von Stromer.

● **However those fossils**, kept in Munich Museum, Germany, were destroyed in 1944 by a World War II bombing raid. In 1996, 1998, 2000, 2002 and 2005, more fossils in North Africa were uncovered and identified as *Spinosaurus*.

● **This giant was probably** more than 14 m long and weighed more than 9 tonnes, perhaps as much as 15.

● **It had tall rods** of bone along its back called neural spines, which probably held up a sail-like area of skin, or perhaps a hump of flesh.

● ***Spinosaurus* and other finds** led to a new group of huge hunting dinosaurs being identified, the spinosaurs, which also included *Giganotosaurus*, *Carcharodontosaurus*, *Baryonyx*, *Oxalaia* and *Suchomimus*.

◄ The skull and jaws of Spinosaurus *were long and low, similar in shape to a crocodile and alligator and also to the medium-sized dinosaur* Baryonyx.

Oviraptor

- **Oviraptor was an unusual meat-eater** from the theropod dinosaur group. It lived during the Late Cretaceous Period, about 75 mya.

- **Its fossils were found** in the Omnogov region of the Gobi Desert in Central Asia.

- **From beak to tail**, *Oviraptor* was about 2 m long.

- **It was named 'egg thief'** because its fossils were found lying among the broken eggs of what was thought to be the dinosaur *Protoceratops*. In fact they were probably the eggs of *Oviraptor* itself, the adult brooding or protecting them.

- **Oviraptor had no teeth**. Instead, it had a strong, curved beak, like that of a parrot or eagle.

- **On its forehead**, *Oviraptor* had a tall, rounded piece of bone, like a crest or helmet, sticking up in front of its eyes.

- **Oviraptor's head crest** resembled that of today's flightless bird, the cassowary.

- **Oviraptor may have eaten eggs**, or cracked open shellfish with its powerful beak.

▼ Oviraptor's *unusual features included its parrot-like beak. It may have been covered in filament-like feathers.*

DID YOU KNOW?

Oviraptor *had two bony spikes inside its mouth that it may have used to crack eggs when it closed its jaws.*

Caudipteryx

- **The discovery of Caudipteryx fossils** in 1997 in Liaoning Province, China, increased the debate about the relationship between dinosaurs and birds.

- **The detailed fossils show** *Caudipteryx* was not much larger than a chicken and had a very bird-like shape and proportions.

- **They also revealed feathers** like a modern bird's, each with a shaft or quill and side vanes, on its front limbs and tail.

- **Some of these feathers** were up to 20 cm long.

- **There were also simple**, fluffy feathers on the body of *Caudipteryx*.

- **The fossils of Caudipteryx** come from 125 mya during the Early Cretaceous Period.

- **There are several views** about the grouping of *Caudipteryx*. Some experts say it is a small meat-eating dinosaur in the same group as *Oviraptor*, related to the raptors.

- **Another opinion** is that it is a dinosaur-like bird, rather than a bird-like dinosaur.

- **The front limbs and build** of *Caudipteryx* meant it could not fly.

- **Caudipteryx could have come from** a group of birds that evolved flight, of which some kinds became flightless again.

◄ Caudipteryx, *meaning 'tail feather', was about one metre long and weighed 5–8 kg. At the end of the tail the long quilled feathers spread out like a fan.*

Smallest dinosaurs

- **One of the smallest** dinosaurs was *Compsognathus*, which lived in the Late Jurassic Period, 155–150 mya.

- **Its fossils** come from Europe, especially southern Germany and southeastern France.

- ***Compsognathus* was probably** just over one metre long and may have weighed less than 3 kg.

- **It had small, sharp, curved teeth** and it probably darted through the undergrowth after insects, spiders, worms and similar small prey.

- **Discovered in 2004** in China, *Mei* was just 50 cm long. It is not only one of the smallest dinosaurs ever found, it also has the shortest dinosaur name of just three letters.

- ***Mei* was fossilized** in a bird-like position with its head bent to one side under its front limb or 'arm', just like a bird tucks its head under its wing when asleep.

▲ *The tiny dinosaur* Mei. *Its full name,* Mei long, *means 'soundly sleeping dragon'.*

◄ *About half of the length of* Compsognathus *was its tail.*

- **The smallest fossil dinosaur specimens** found to date are of *Mussaurus*, which means 'mouse reptile'. The fossils were of babies, just 20 cm long, newly hatched from eggs. The babies would have grown into adults measuring 3 m in length.

- **Two other small dinosaurs** were the 60-cm-long *Caenagnathasia* and the 40-cm-long *Parvicursor*.

Pack hunters

- **Dinosaurs were reptiles**, but no reptiles today hunt in packs in which members co-operate with each other.

- **Certain types of crocodiles** and alligators come together to feed where prey is abundant, but they do not co-ordinate their attacks.

- **Fossil evidence suggests** that several kinds of meat-eating dinosaurs hunted in groups or packs.

- **Sometimes the fossils** of several individuals of the same type of dinosaur have been found in one place, suggesting the dinosaurs were pack animals.

- **The fossil bones** of some plant-eating dinosaurs have been found with many tooth marks on them, apparently made by different-sized predators, which may have hunted in packs.

- ***Tyrannosaurus*** may have been a pack hunter.

- **At several North American sites**, the remains of several *Deinonychus* were found near the fossils of a much larger plant-eater named *Tenontosaurus*.

- **One *Deinonychus*** probably would not have attacked a full-grown *Tenontosaurus*, but a group of three or four might have.

◄ *Small predatory dinosaurs such as* Troodon *may have gathered in groups to chase prey or scavenge.*

Raptors

- **'Raptors' is a nickname for** the dromaeosaur group. It is variously said to mean 'plunderer', 'thief' or 'hunter' (birds of prey are also called raptors).

- **Dromaeosaurs were** medium- to large-sized, powerful, agile, meat-eating dinosaurs that lived mainly about 110–66 mya.

▶ Velociraptor, *the 'speedy thief', was a typical dromaeosaur. Fossils of it were found in Central Asia. Most raptors probably had feathers, although for some there is no direct fossil evidence.*

- **Most dromaeosaurs** were 1.5–3 m from nose to tail, weighed 20–60 kg, and stood 1–2 m tall.

- **Velociraptor lived** 75–70 mya, in what is now the barren scrub and desert of Mongolia in Central Asia.

- **Like other raptors**, Velociraptor probably ran fast and could leap great distances on its powerful back legs.

- **The dromaeosaurs** are named after the 1.8-m-long *Dromaeosaurus* of North America – one of the least known of the group, from very few fossil finds.

- **The most-studied raptor** is probably *Deinonychus*.

- **The large mouths** of dromaeosaurs opened wide and were equipped with small, sharp, curved teeth.

DID YOU KNOW?

On each second toe, a dromaeosaur had a large, curved claw that it could swing in an arc to slash through its victim's flesh.

Deinonychus

- **Deinonychus** is one of the best known raptors.

- **It thrived** in the Middle Cretaceous Period, about 115–105 mya.

- **Fossils of Deinonychus** come from the American Midwest, mainly from Montana and Wyoming.

- **Deinonychus was about 3–3.5 m long** from nose to tail and weighed 60–70 kg, about the same as an adult human.

- **When remains of Deinonychus** were dug up and studied in the 1960s, they exploded the myth that dinosaurs were slow, small-brained and stupid.

- **Powerful, speedy and agile**, Deinonychus may have hunted in packs, like today's lions and wolves.

- **It had large hands** with three powerful fingers, each tipped with a dangerous sharp claw.

◀ *There is no direct fossil evidence for feathers in* Deinonychus, *but remains of many other raptor-type dinosaurs show feathers of various kinds, not for flight, but perhaps for insulation or display.*

- **Deinonychus also had** the massive, scythe-like claw, typical of the raptor group, on each second toe.

- **The tail was stiff** and could not be swished.

- **Deinonychus and other similar dromaeosaurs**, such as *Velociraptor*, were the basis for the cunning and terrifying raptors of the *Jurassic Park* films.

Utahraptor

● **The finding of** *Utahraptor* fossils dates back to 1975 near Moab, Utah, USA, but these caused little excitement.

● **More fossils** from the early 1990s were added to the discovery and dated to about 130–125 mya, the Early Cretaceous Period.

● **By 1993** enough remains had been identified to name this new medium-sized meat-eater *Utahraptor*.

● **It was one of the biggest members** of the raptor or dromaeosaur group, far larger than *Velociraptor* and *Deinonychus*.

● *Utahraptor* **measured** about 7 m long and weighed up to 420 kg.

● **Like other raptors**, it was fast and powerful, with a fearsome curved claw on each foot.

● **One of these claws** was more than 22 cm long. It could swing on its flexible toe in a slashing or slicing movement to wound prey.

● **Preserved feathers** have not been found with *Utahraptor* remains, but since many of its close relatives had them, it may have possessed feathers, too.

● **The full name is** *Utahraptor ostrommaysorum*, partly in honour of the US palaeontologist John Ostrom whose work on *Deinonychus* did so much to change people's opinions of dinosaurs.

▼ *The main fossils of Utahraptor were excavated following the discovery of its huge foot claw in a quarry in Utah, USA.*

Gigantoraptor

● *Gigantoraptor* **was certainly very large**, but it was not a member of the raptor or dromaeosaur group of fast meat-eating dinosaurs.

● **Instead it belonged** to the bird-like group called oviraptors, named after the much smaller *Oviraptor*.

● *Gigantoraptor* **has been compared** to a massive chicken, standing more than 3 m tall, with a length of 7–8 m and a weight of 1.5 tonnes.

● **It had toothless jaws** that in life were probably covered by a big, strong beak.

● **The legs of** *Gigantoraptor* were long and strong for fast running, and the toes ended in big claws.

● **From its size and skull**, *Gigantoraptor* was probably a herbivore, pecking at plant matter. Or it had a wider diet including bugs, eggs and small animals, being an omnivore.

● *Gigantoraptor* **lived about 70 mya**, near the very end of the Age of Dinosaurs.

▶ Gigantoraptor *fossils were found in 2007 and officially named two years later. This dinosaur may have been an omnivore, pecking up all kinds of food like an oversized modern ostrich.*

> ## DID YOU KNOW?
>
> Signs of fossil eggs from the area where Gigantoraptor was found (Mongolia) suggest it may have laid eggs more than 45 cm long.

Feathered dinosaurs

- **Fossils found** since the mid-1990s show that some dinosaurs may have been covered with feathers or fur.

- *Sinosauropteryx* **was a small**, one-metre-long meat-eater that lived 125–120 mya in China.

- **Fossils of** *Sinosauropteryx* show that parts of its body were covered not with the usual reptile scales, but with feathers instead.

▶ Avimimus *may have evolved feathers for warmth, keeping cool, camouflage, display, to shield its eggs on the nest – or a combination of all these.*

- **The overall shape** of *Sinosauropteryx* shows that, despite being feathered, it could not fly.

- **The feathers may have been** for camouflage, for visual display, or to keep it warm – suggesting it was warm-blooded.

- **Fossils of** *Avimimus* come from China and Mongolia, and date from about 75–70 mya.

- **The fossil arm bones** have small ridges that are the same size and shape as the ridges on birds' wing bones, where feathers attach.

- **The 1.5-m-long** *Avimimus* had a mouth shaped like a bird's beak for pecking at food.

- **Most scientists today** believe that birds are descended from a group of small meat-eating dinosaurs called maniraptorans, such as *Troodon*.

- **If this is so**, the modern way of classifying animals, called cladistics, means that birds are a subgroup of dinosaurs, not a separate group. That in turn means that dinosaurs exist today – in the form of birds.

Microraptor

- *Microraptor* **is one of the smallest** and most feathered dinosaurs ever found.

- **It probably weighed** less than one kilogram and was only 80–90 cm long.

- **Its fossils are 125–120 million years old** and come from the Liaoning area of northeast China.

- **Finds so far** are of more than 250 specimens, making *Microraptor* one of the most common creatures at that time.

- *Microraptor* **was probably** a raptor in the dromaeosaur group.

- **It was also 'four-winged'** – it had feathers on its arms and legs.

- **These feathers were up to 20 cm long** on the arms, 15 cm on the legs, and well designed for flight.

- **Simpler**, plume-like feathers were on the tail.

- **It is not clear** whether *Microraptor* was an extremely good glider, swooping down skilfully from trees, or whether it could truly fly in a controlled, sustained way, like a bird.

◀ Microraptor *was the first known 'four-winged dinosaur', receiving its official name in 2000.*

- **The feathers meant** *Microraptor* would have had problems walking and running on the ground, so it probably lived in trees.

DID YOU KNOW?

Fossils of several Microraptor contain small bones and other parts from mammals, birds, lizards and even fish, which were probably their last meals.

Xiaotingia

- **Xiaotingia** was a tiny, bird-like dinosaur (probably) belonging to the dromaeosaur or raptor group.

- **It is one of the earlier feathered dinosaurs**, dating from about 160–150 mya, towards the end of the Jurassic Period – before the time of the famed bird *Archaeopteryx*.

- **Fossils of Xiaotingia** were found in Liaoning, China and named in 2011.

- **The remains consist** of most of one skeleton, although parts of the pelvis, one leg and most of the tail bones are missing, but with feather impressions present.

- **In life**, *Xiaotingia* was around 60 cm long and weighed some 2 kg. It probably ate small bugs, insects and worms.

- **Some features of Xiaotingia** are very similar to those of *Archaeopteryx*, including the feathers, claws on its arms – or wings – and teeth in its jaws.

- **This led some experts to declare** that *Archaeopteryx* was not a bird at all, but a bird-like type of dinosaur.

▲ Xiaotingia, *named in honour of Chinese fossil expert Zheng Xiaoting, was probably capable of a certain amount of controlled flight, but was not as agile as today's birds.*

- **Other experts suggested** *Xiaotingia* was not a dinosaur but a bird, and since it lived before *Archaeopteryx*, *Xiaotingia* should take its place as the earliest bird known from fossils.

- **Such debates demonstrate** how similar dromaeosaur dinosaurs and early birds were, and may cause us to revise our definitions of what a bird is in the future.

Ostrich dinosaurs

- **'Ostrich dinosaurs'** is the common name of the ornithomimosaurs, because of their resemblance to today's largest bird – the flightless ostrich.

- **These dinosaurs** were tall and slim, with two long, powerful back legs for running fast.

- **The front limbs** were like strong arms, with grasping fingers tipped by sharp claws.

- **The eyes were large** and set high on the head.

- **The toothless mouth** was similar to the long, slim beak of a bird.

DID YOU KNOW?

Fossils of front limbs found in 1965, and named Deinocheirus, indicate a huge ostrich dinosaur 10 m long, 4 m tall, and 5 tonnes in weight.

- **Ostrich dinosaurs** lived towards the end of the Cretaceous Period, about 100–66 mya, in North America and Asia.

- **Fossils of the ostrich dinosaur** *Struthiomimus* from Alberta, Canada, suggest it was almost 4 m in total length and stood about 2 m tall – the same height as a modern ostrich.

- **The ostrich dinosaur** *Gallimimus* was almost 8 m long and stood nearly 3 m high.

- **Ostrich dinosaurs** probably ate seeds, fruits and other plant material, as well as small animals such as worms and lizards, which they may have grasped with their powerful clawed hands.

- **Other ostrich dinosaurs** included *Dromiceiomimus*, at 3–4 m long, and the slightly bigger *Ornithomimus*.

◄ Ornithomimus *could reach speeds of perhaps 80 km/h when running. It had strong muscles in its hips and legs, enabling it to take long, quick strides.*

Therizinosaurs

- **For years**, finds of huge fossil claws puzzled experts as to which creatures they came from.

- **In the 1990s** more finds made the picture clearer. They came from a previously unknown dinosaur group, related to meat-eaters, but plant-eaters themselves.

- **The new group was named in 1997** as the therizinosaurs, 'scythe lizards' or 'reaper lizards', after their massively long claws.

- **A less-used name** is segnosaurs – 'slow lizards'.

- **Therizinosaurs belonged** to the theropod group, in which all the other kinds were meat-eaters, from tiny raptors to giants like *Tyrannosaurus* and *Spinosaurus*.

- **But the skulls and teeth** of therizinosaurs show they were probably plant-eaters.

- **Most therizinosaurs stood** on their back legs, had wide hips, feathers and were large. Some were enormous – *Therizinosaurus* itself stood 5 m tall, was 10 m long, and weighed 5 tonnes.

- **Most therizinosaur fossils** come from the Middle and Late Cretaceous Period, 130–66 mya, and are found in East Asia, with some from North America.

- *Alaxasaurus* **was one** of the smaller therizinosaurs, about 2.2 m tall and 3.5 m long.

- **Its discovery** helped to establish the group, and show it was a subgroup of the theropods, whose close relatives were the bird-like raptors and oviraptors.

▼ *Therizinosaurus was one of the last of its group, surviving about 70 mya in what is now Mongolia, Central Asia. Its first fossils, giant claws, were found in the 1940s but remained a mystery for almost half a century.*

Falcarius

- *Falcarius* **was a therizinosaur** that lived in what is now Utah, USA, around 125 mya.

- **It is one of the earliest known** therizinosaurs, or 'scythe lizards', and shows how the group evolved from other kinds of theropods.

- **Thousands of fossil specimens** from hundreds of individuals, of various sizes and ages, have been recovered, making this dinosaur very well known.

- *Falcarius* **was up to 4 m long** and 1.2 m tall, and weighed about 100 kg.

- **Some of the smallest**, youngest individuals were only 50 cm long.

- *Falcarius* **had leaf-shaped teeth** in its upper jaw, similar to those of plant-eating dinosaurs such as sauropods.

- **Some of its teeth** in the front of the lower jaw were more spike-shaped, perhaps showing *Falcarius* could also catch animals like insects and small reptiles.

- **Like other therizinosaurs**, *Falcarius* had hugely elongated claws on each hand.

- *Falcarius* **fossils** were first noticed in 1999, and it was officially described and named in 2005.

- **No feathers have been found** preserved with *Falcarius* bones and teeth, showing that perhaps they had not yet evolved in this group.

▶ *Falcarius, 'sickle slicer', had the typical therizinosaur claws on its hands, measuring 10–14 cm in length.*

DID YOU KNOW?

Since 2000, thousands of fossilized bones of Falcarius have been found in quarries in Utah, USA. There are also bits of skull and hundreds of claws.

Herbivores

● **Many dinosaurs** were herbivores, or plant-eaters. As time passed, the plants available for them to eat evolved, and new dinosaurs adapted to eat them.

● **Early in the Age of Dinosaurs**, during the Triassic Period, the main plants for dinosaurs to eat were conifer trees, ginkgoes, cycads and the smaller seed ferns, ferns, horsetails and club mosses.

● **A few cycads** are still found today. They resemble palm trees, with umbrella-like crowns of long green fronds on top of tall, unbranched, trunk-like stems.

● **In the Triassic Period**, only prosauropod dinosaurs were big enough or had necks long enough to reach tall cycad fronds or ginkgo leaves.

● **In the Jurassic Period**, tall conifers such as redwoods and araucarias or 'monkey puzzle' trees became common.

● **The huge, long-necked sauropods** of the Jurassic Period may have been able to reach high into tall conifer trees to rake off their needles.

● **In the Middle Cretaceous Period**, a new type of plant food appeared – the flowering plants.

▼ *During the warm, damp Jurassic Period, plants grew in most areas, covering land that previously had been barren. Massive plant-eaters such as Barosaurus thrived on the fronds, needles and leaves of towering tree ferns, ginkgoes and conifers.*

● **By the end of the Cretaceous Period** there were many flowering trees and shrubs, such as magnolias, maples and walnuts.

● **These new plants** meant that many new kinds of animals, including new herbivorous dinosaurs, evolved to eat them.

Lesothosaurus and Fabrosaurus

● **There has been much confusion** between two very small plant-eating dinosaurs, *Lesothosaurus* and *Fabrosaurus*.

● **Their fossils come from South Africa** and date back to the Early Jurassic Period, 200–190 mya.

● ***Fabrosaurus* was named** in 1964 from just one fossil specimen of three teeth, set in part of a jawbone.

● **Comparing this specimen** with similar fossils, these indicated a plant-eater about one metre long.

● ***Lesothosaurus* was named** in 1978. Its fossils showed a one-metre plant-eater similar to *Fabrosaurus*.

● **Slim and light**, *Lesothosaurus* would have stood knee-high to a person.

● **Long, slim back legs** and toes indicate that *Lesothosaurus* was a fast runner.

● **Teeth and other fossils** of *Lesothosaurus* show that it probably ate low-growing plants such as ferns.

● **The rear teeth were set inwards** slightly from the sides of its skull, suggesting fleshy cheek pouches for storing or chewing food.

● **It is possible that** *Lesothosaurus* and *Fabrosaurus* were the same type of dinosaur. If so, all the fossils should receive the name given first – *Fabrosaurus*.

● **But *Fabrosaurus*** remains are so limited, some experts say it should not even exist as an official name.

● ***Lesothosaurus* may be** an early type of ornithischian or 'bird-hipped' dinosaur, perhaps on the way to becoming an ornithopod like *Iguanodon* – or a stegosaur or ankylosaur.

▼ Lesothosaurus *may have stood on hind legs to spot danger, much like the mammals called meerkats in the region today.*

Prosauropods

- **The first big dinosaurs** were the prosauropods, also called plateosaurids. Most lived between 230 and 180 mya.

- **They were plant-eaters**, with small heads, long necks and tails, wide bodies and four sturdy limbs.

- **One of the first prosauropods** was *Plateosaurus*, which lived in Europe between 215–205 mya.

▼ Riojasaurus *was South America's first big dinosaur.*

- *Plateosaurus* **walked on all fours**, but may have reared up on its back legs to reach leaves. It was up to 9 m long, and weighed as much as 3 tonnes.

- **Another prosauropod** was *Riojasaurus*. Its fossils are about 220–215 million years old, and come from Argentina.

- *Riojasaurus* **was 10 m long** and weighed about 2 tonnes.

- **Over 20 fossil skeletons** of the prosauropod *Sellosaurus* have been found in Europe, dating from 215–210 mya.

- *Lufengosaurus* was an early Jurassic prosauropod from China, measuring up to 9 m in length. It was the first complete dinosaur skeleton to be restored in that country.

- **The sauropods** followed the prosauropods and were even bigger, but had the same basic body shape, with long necks and tails.

DID YOU KNOW?

A close relative of Riojasaurus was Melanorosaurus from Africa – South America and Africa were once joined as part of Gondwana, 200 mya.

Plateosaurus

- **The name *Plateosaurus*** means 'flat reptile', and the first kinds appeared around 215 mya.

- **Groups of *Plateosaurus*** have been found at various European sites, totalling more than 100 individuals.

- *Plateosaurus* **had jagged teeth** for chewing plant matter.

- **Its flexible, clawed fingers** may have been used to pull branches of food to its mouth.

- *Plateosaurus* **could bend** its fingers 'backwards', allowing it to walk on its hands and fingers, in the same posture as its feet and toes.

- **The thumbs** had large, sharp claws, perhaps used to jab and stab enemies.

- **Fossil experts once thought** that *Plateosaurus* dragged its tail as it walked.

- **Experts today think** that *Plateosaurus* carried its tail off the ground to balance its head, neck and the front part of its body.

- *Plateosaurus* was one of the earliest dinosaurs to be officially named, in 1837, even before the term 'dinosaur' had been invented.

▼ Plateosaurus *may have been able to reach leaves 2–3 m above the ground.*

Massospondylus

● **Massospondylus was a medium-sized** plant-eater belonging to the group known as the prosauropods.

● **Africa and perhaps North America** were home to Massospondylus, about 200–185 mya.

● **In total**, Massospondylus was about 4.5 m long, with almost half of this length being its tail.

● **The rear legs** of Massospondylus were bigger and stronger than its front legs, so it may have reared up to reach food high up.

● **The name Massospondylus** means 'huge backbone'.

● **Fossils of over 80 Massospondylus** have been found, making it one of the best-studied dinosaurs.

● **Massospondylus had a tiny head** compared to its body, so it must have spent hours each day gathering enough food to survive.

● **The front teeth** of Massospondylus were large and strong with ridged edges.

● **The cheek teeth** were too small and weak to chew large amounts of food, so perhaps food was mashed in the dinosaur's stomach.

● **In the 1980s**, some scientists suggested that Massospondylus was a meat-eater, partly due to its ridged front teeth, but this idea is now outdated.

DID YOU KNOW?

Massospondylus was named in 1854 by palaeontologist Richard Owen. He thought at first the fossils came from three different reptiles.

◄ Massospondylus *probably spent most of its time eating to fuel its bulky body.*

Anchisaurus

● **Anchisaurus** was an early sauropod-like dinosaur.

● **Although officially named** in 1885, Anchisaurus had in fact been discovered over 70 years earlier.

● **Anchisaurus was very small** and slim compared to other sauropods, with a body about the size of a large dog.

● **Fossils of Anchisaurus** date from the Early Jurassic Period, 200–190 mya.

● **The remains of Anchisaurus** were found in Connecticut and Massachusetts, eastern USA, and in southern Africa.

● **With its small, serrated teeth**, Anchisaurus probably bit off the soft leaves of low-growing plants.

● **To reach leaves** on higher branches, Anchisaurus may have been able to rear up on its back legs.

● **Anchisaurus had a large**, curved claw on each thumb.

● **The thumb claws** may have been used as hooks to pull leafy branches towards the mouth, or as weapons for lashing out at enemies and inflicting wounds.

▲ Anchisaurus *was about 2.2 m long. Its name means 'near lizard'.*

Biggest dinosaurs

- **Dinosaurs can be measured** by length and height, but 'biggest' usually means heaviest or bulkiest.

- **The sauropod dinosaurs** of the Late Jurassic and Early–Mid Cretaceous Periods were the biggest animals to walk on Earth, as far as we know.

- **However, today's whales**, and maybe the huge sea reptiles (pliosaurs) of the Dinosaur Age, rival them in size.

- **For any dinosaur**, enough fossils must be found for scientists to be sure it is a distinct type before they can give it a scientific name. They must also be able to estimate its size. With some giant dinosaurs, not enough fossils have been found.

- **Remains of *Supersaurus*** found in Colorado, USA, suggest a dinosaur similar to *Diplodocus*, but perhaps even longer, at 35 m.

- ***Diplodocus hallorum* fossils** found in 1991 in the USA may belong to a 35-m-long sauropod.

- ***Ultrasaurus* fossils** found in South Korea suggest a dinosaur similar to *Brachiosaurus*, but smaller. However these fossils are fragmentary and some experts disagree with their naming.

- ***Argentinosaurus***, from South America, is known from a few fossils, mainly backbones, found in the early 1990s. It may have weighed up to 100 tonnes.

◄ Seismosaurus was named in 1991, but further studies in the 2000s show it was probably one of the species of Diplodocus, now known as Diplodocus hallorum or Diplodocus longus.

Sauropods

- **Sauropods were the biggest dinosaurs** of all. They lived mainly during the Jurassic Period, around 201–145 mya.

- **These huge plant-eaters** had tiny heads, very long necks and tails, huge, bulging bodies and massive legs, similar to those of an elephant, but much bigger.

- **Sauropods included** the well known *Mamenchisaurus*, *Cetiosaurus*, *Diplodocus*, *Brachiosaurus* and *Apatosaurus*.

- ***Rebbachisaurus* fossils** were found in Morocco, Tunisia and Algeria. It lived 100 mya.

- ***Cetiosaurus* was about** 15 m long and weighed 10–20 tonnes.

- **The first fossils** of *Cetiosaurus* were found in Oxfordshire, England, in the 1830s. It was the first sauropod to be given an official name, in 1841 – the year before the term 'dinosaur' was invented.

- ***Cetiosaurus***, or 'whale reptile', was so-named because British fossil expert Richard Owen thought that its giant backbones came from a prehistoric whale.

DID YOU KNOW?

'Sauropod' means 'lizard/ reptile foot'. It was given in 1878 by US fossil hunter Othniel Charles Marsh, after the discovery of Diplodocus.

► Sauropods such as Apatosaurus could perhaps browse for food in tree tops.

Brachiosaurus

- *Brachiosaurus* **lived about 155–150 mya** and its fossils have been found at several sites in North America. Fossils of a similar dinosaur from Africa, previously thought to have been *Brachiosaurus*, have been renamed *Giraffatitan*.

- **At 25 m in length** from nose to tail, *Brachiosaurus* was not one of the longest dinosaurs, but it was one of the heaviest. Its weight has been estimated between 20 and 50 tonnes.

- *Brachiosaurus* **fossils** were first found in 1900 and the dinosaur was named the year after.

- **The name** *Brachiosaurus* means 'arm reptile' – it was so-named because of its massive front legs.

- **With its huge front legs** and long neck, *Brachiosaurus* could perhaps reach food more than 13 m from the ground.

- **Its teeth were small** and chisel-shaped for snipping leaves from trees. The nostrils were positioned high on its head.

▶ Brachiosaurus *had similar body proportions to a giraffe, but was more than twice as tall and 50 times heavier.*

Camarasaurus

- *Camarasaurus* **was an enormous** plant-eating sauropod that lived during the Late Jurassic Period, about 155–150 mya.

- **It is one of the best known** of all big dinosaurs, because so many almost-complete fossil skeletons have been found.

- **Famous American fossil hunter** Edward Drinker Cope gave *Camarasaurus* its name in 1877.

- **The name means** 'chambered reptile', because its backbones, or vertebrae, had large, scoop-shaped spaces in them, making them lighter.

▼ Compared to other sauropods, Camarasaurus *had a short neck and tail.*

- *Camarasaurus* was up to 21 m long and had a very bulky, powerful body and legs.

- **North America was home** to *Camarasaurus*, with similar fossils from Europe and Africa given different names.

- **A large, short-snouted head**, similar to that of *Brachiosaurus*, characterized *Camarasaurus*.

- **A fossil skeleton** of a young *Camarasaurus* was uncovered in the 1920s, and had nearly every bone in its body lying in the correct position, as they were when the dinosaur was alive – an amazingly rare find.

DID YOU KNOW?

Fossil studies show that one Camarasaurus replaced its teeth every 8–9 weeks, and another reached adulthood at 20 years and died aged 26.

Brontomerus

- **Brontomerus is a recently named sauropod** dinosaur whose fossils come from a quarry in Utah, USA.

- **The fossils are from** about 100 mya, towards the end of the Early Cretaceous Period, or the Middle Cretaceous.

- **The fossil fragments indicate** a medium-sized sauropod about 14 m long, weighing 5–6 tonnes, and similar in looks to the much better-known *Camarasaurus*.

- **The name Brontomerus means** 'thunder thigh' and refers to the very unusual, large hip bones, which would have anchored hugely powerful hip and thigh muscles for the rear legs.

- **Another 'bronto' was Brontosaurus**, 'thunder lizard', which used to be a very famous dinosaur name.

- **It was given in 1897** by fossil-hunter Othniel Charles Marsh to fossils of a large sauropod from the Midwest of the USA.

- **Two years before**, Marsh had named another similar sauropod, about 23 m long and weighing 20 tonnes, as *Apatosaurus*.

► *The pelvic (hip) bones and femur (thigh bone) of Brontomerus had large surfaces to anchor bulky, powerful muscles.*

► *The muscle marks on the fossil limb bones of Brontomerus show that it could probably kick very hard with its rear legs.*

- **Later studies of these fossils** showed that those named *Brontosaurus* were in fact the same kind of dinosaur as *Apatosaurus*.

- **So the first specimens** known as *Brontosaurus* were renamed *Apatosaurus*, and *Brontosaurus* was dropped from the official list of dinosaur names.

Mamenchisaurus

- **A massive plant-eating dinosaur**, *Mamenchisaurus* was similar in appearance to *Diplodocus*.

- **It lived during** the late Jurassic Period, from 160–145 mya.

- **This huge dinosaur** measured about 30 m from nose to tail. Its weight has been estimated at 20–35 tonnes.

- **At up to 15 m**, *Mamenchisaurus* had one of the longest necks of any dinosaur. The neck had up to 19 vertebrae, or neckbones – more than almost any other dinosaur.

- **The remains of Mamenchisaurus** were found in China and the dinosaur is named after the place where its fossils were discovered – Mamen Stream.

- **Other sauropod dinosaurs** found in the same region include *Euhelopus* and *Omeisaurus*.

- **Mamenchisaurus may have stretched** out its neck to crop leaves, or – less likely – may have lived in swamps and eaten water plants.

▲ *The joints between the fossil bones of Mamenchisaurus' neck show that it was not very flexible.*

DID YOU KNOW?

Five or six more possible species of Mamenchisaurus have been identified – although some experts say the remains represent two or three species.

Super sauropods

The sauropods were the largest dinosaurs and the biggest land animals that have ever lived. All sauropods were plant-eaters. They had massive bodies with long, slender necks and tails and relatively small heads. The legs were straight and thick so that they could support the huge weight of these animals. There were many different types of sauropod, but they all had the same basic appearance. Some sauropods had bone armour plates set into their skin, others had bone clubs on their tails. These may have helped defend the creatures against hunter dinosaurs. A few sauropods may have had spines growing along their backs that might have supported a colourful flap of skin.

SAUROPOD SIZE COMPARISON

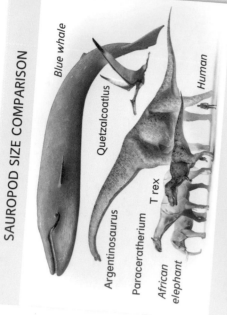

Blue whale

Quetzalcoatlus

Argentinosaurus

Paraceratherium

T rex

Human

African elephant

At 180 tonnes the blue whale is the biggest animal ever. With a wingspan of over 10 m, *Quetzalcoatlus* was a huge pterosaur. *Argentinosaurus* was a huge sauropod weighing 83 tonnes. *T rex* was a hefty 6 tonnes, and *Paraceratherium* was the largest land mammal at 20 tonnes. The African elephant is the biggest modern land animal at 6 tonnes.

▼ **BROWSING HIGH**
Some sauropods, such as Brachiosaurus, may have reared up on their hind legs, using their tails for support. This may have helped them reach food.

▼ **GRAZING LOW**
By swinging their necks from side to side, sauropods may have been able to eat ground plants from a wide area without moving their bodies too far.

Sauropods first appeared about 210 million years ago in the Late Triassic Period. The largest types lived in the later Jurassic Period, about 150 million years ago, when the sauropods were most numerous. A few kinds survived until the end of the Age of Dinosaurs, about 65 million years ago.

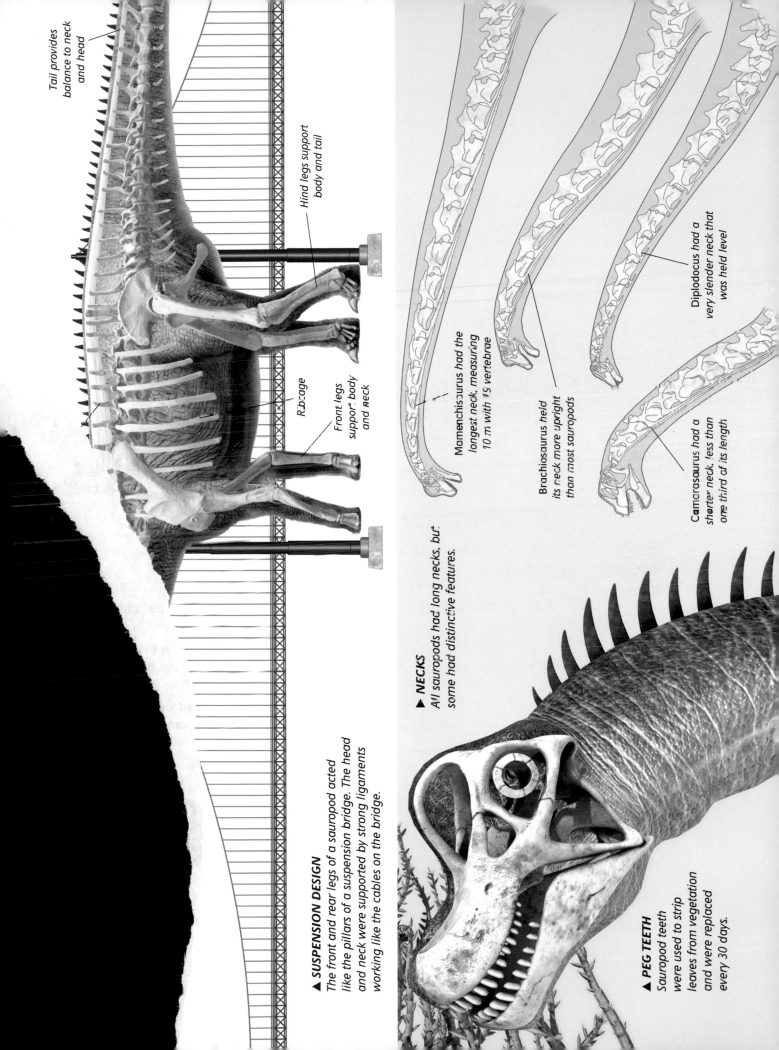

Tail provides balance to neck and head

Hind legs support body and tail

Rib cage

Front legs support body and neck

▲ SUSPENSION DESIGN
The front and rear legs of a sauropod acted like the pillars of a suspension bridge. The head and neck were supported by strong ligaments working like the cables on the bridge.

▲ NECKS
All sauropods had long necks, but some had distinctive features.

Mamenchisaurus had the longest neck, measuring 10 m with 19 vertebrae

Brachiosaurus held its neck more upright than most sauropods

Diplodocus had a very slender neck that was held level

Camarasaurus had a shorter neck, less than one third of its length

▲ PEG TEETH
Sauropod teeth were used to strip leaves from vegetation and were replaced every 30 days.

Stegosaurus

- *Stegosaurus* **was the largest** of the stegosaur group. Its fossils were found mainly in present-day Colorado, Utah and Wyoming, USA.

- **Like most of its group**, *Stegosaurus* lived towards the end of the Jurassic Period, about 155–150 mya.

- *Stegosaurus* **was about 8–9 m long** from nose to tail and probably weighed more than 4 tonnes.

- **Its most striking features** were the large, roughly diamond-shaped, leaf-shaped or triangular bony plates along its back.

- **The name** *Stegosaurus* means 'roof reptile'. This is because it was first thought that its bony plates lay flat on its back, overlapping like the tiles on a roof.

- **It is now thought** that the back plates stood upright in two long rows.

- **The plates may have been** for body temperature control, allowing the dinosaur to warm up quickly if it stood side-on to the sun's rays.

- **The back plates** may have been covered with brightly coloured skin, possibly to intimidate enemies – they were too flimsy to provide much protection.

- **Armed with four large spikes**, *Stegosaurus* probably used its tail for swinging at enemies in self-defence.

◀ *Stegosaurus' short front limbs meant that it ate low-growing plants.*

DID YOU KNOW?

When Stegosaurus fossils were first found in 1876–77, they were thought to be of a sea turtle, with the back plates lying flat to form the shell.

Tuojiangosaurus

- *Tuojiangosaurus* **was part** of the stegosaur group. It lived during the Late Jurassic Period, about 170–155 mya.

- **The first nearly complete** dinosaur skeleton to be found in China was of a *Tuojiangosaurus*, and fossil skeletons are on display in several Chinese museums.

- **The name** *Tuojiangosaurus* means 'Tuo River reptile'.

- *Tuojiangosaurus* **was 7 m long** from nose to tail and probably weighed about 3–4 tonnes.

- **Like other stegosaurs**, *Tuojiangosau[r]* plates of bone on its back.

- **The back plates** were roughly tria[ngular] probably stood upright in two rows th[at ran from the] neck to the middle of the tail.

- *Tuojiangosaurus* **plucked** lo[w-growing plants with] its beak-shaped mouth, and part[ly chewed them with its] ridged cheek teeth.

◀ *Tuojiangosaurus ha[d ... spikes on] its tail that it swung at e[nemies.]*

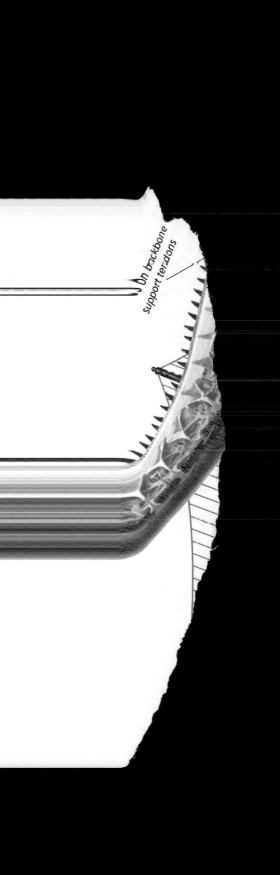

on backbone
support tendons

Ankylosaurs

- **Ankylosaurs** had a protective armour of bony plates.

- **Unlike the armoured nodosaurs**, ankylosaurs had a large lump of bone at the end of their tail, which they used as a hammer or club.

- **One of the best known ankylosaurs**, from the preserved remains of about 40 individuals, is *Euoplocephalus*.

- **The hefty** *Euoplocephalus* was about 6 m long and weighed 2 tonnes or more. It lived about 76–75 mya in Alberta, Canada, Montana, USA and other places.

- *Euoplocephalus* **had bony shields** on its head and body, and even had bony eyelids. Blunt spikes ran along its back.

- **Specimens of** *Euoplocephalus* are usually found singly, so it probably didn't live in herds.

- **The ankylosaur** *Pinacosaurus* had bony nodules like chainmail armour in its skin, and rows of blunt spikes from neck to tail.

- **Ankylosaurs had small**, weak teeth, and probably ate soft, low-growing ferns and horsetails.

> **DID YOU KNOW?**
> *Pinacosaurus was about 5 m long and lived in Asia some 80–75 mya.*

▶ *The tail club of Euoplocephalus was made from pieces of bone that had fused (stuck) together.*

Scelidosaurus

- **Scelidosaurus was** a medium-sized armoured dinosaur, perhaps an early member of the ankylosaur or stegosaur group.

- **Very well-preserved fossils** of *Scelidosaurus* have been found in Dorset, in southern England. It lived during the Early Jurassic Period, about 190 mya.

- **From nose to tail**, *Scelidosaurus* was about 4 m long.

- *Scelidosaurus* **probably** moved about on four legs, although it could perhaps rear up to gather food.

- **A plant-eater**, *Scelidosaurus* snipped off food with the beak-like front of its mouth, and chewed with its simple, leaf-shaped teeth.

- *Scelidosaurus* **is one of the earliest** dinosaurs known to have had a set of protective, bony armour plates.

◀ *Scelidosaurus was a forerunner of bigger, more heavily armoured dinosaur types, with bony plates called scutes.*

- **A row of bony plates**, or scutes, stuck up from *Scelidosaurus'* neck, back and tail. It also had rows of conical bony plates along its flanks, resembling limpets on a rock.

- *Scelidosaurus* **was described** and named in 1859 and 1861 by Richard Owen, who also invented the name 'dinosaur'.

Nodosaurs

- **Nodosaurs were a subgroup** of armoured dinosaurs in the main ankylosaur group.

- **The nodosaur subgroup** included *Edmontonia*, *Sauropelta*, *Polacanthus* and *Nodosaurus*.

- **Nodosaurs were slow-moving**, heavy-bodied plant-eaters with thick, heavy nodules, lumps and plates of bone in their skin for protection.

- **Most nodosaurs lived** during the Late Jurassic and Cretaceous Periods, 160–66 mya.

- *Edmontonia* **lived** in North America during the Late Cretaceous Period, 75–66 mya.

- **It was about 7 m long**, but its bony armour made it very heavy for its size, at 4–5 tonnes.

- **Along its neck**, back and tail *Edmontonia* had rows of flat and spiky plates.

▼ Edmontonia, *one of the last dinosaurs, was covered in many sharp lumps and spikes of bone that gave it some protection from its enemies.*

- **The nodosaur** *Polacanthus* was about 5 m long and lived 130–120 mya.

- **Fossils of** *Polacanthus* come from the Isle of Wight, England, and perhaps from North America, in South Dakota, USA.

Sauropelta

- *Sauropelta* **was a nodosaur** – a type of armoured dinosaur.

- **The name** *Sauropelta* means 'shielded reptile', from the many large, cone-like lumps of bone – some almost as big as dinner plates – on its head, neck, back and tail.

- **The larger lumps of bone** on *Sauropelta* were interspersed with smaller, fist-sized bony studs.

- *Sauropelta* **was about** 5 m long, including the tail, and probably weighed almost 2 tonnes.

- *Sauropelta* **had a row** of sharp spikes along each side of its body, from just behind the eyes to the tail. The spikes decreased in size towards the tail.

- **The armour** of *Sauropelta* was flexible, almost like lumps of metal set into thick leather, so the dinosaur could twist and turn, but was unable to run fast.

- **Pillar-like legs** supported *Sauropelta's* weight.

- **Using its beak-like mouth**, *Sauropelta* probably plucked its low-growing plant food.

▶ *If attacked, Sauropelta probably crouched down low to protect its soft belly. It may have swung its head to jab at enemies with its long neck spines.*

DID YOU KNOW?

Sauropelta lived 115–110 mya, in present-day Montana and Wyoming, USA.

Heterodontosaurus

- *Heterodontosaurus* **lived** about 200–195 mya, at the beginning of the Jurassic Period.

- **A very small dinosaur** at only one metre in length (about as long as a large dog), *Heterodontosaurus* would have stood knee-high to a human.

- **Probably standing partly upright** on its longer back legs, *Heterodontosaurus* would have been a fast runner.

- **Fossils of *Heterodontosaurus*** come from Lesotho in southern Africa and Cape Province in South Africa.

- **The majority of dinosaurs had teeth** of only one shape in their jaws, but *Heterodontosaurus* had three types of teeth.

- **The front teeth** were small, sharp and found only in the upper jaw. They bit against the horny, beak-like lower front of the mouth.

▲ Small and slim, Heterodontosaurus *looked similar to meat-eaters such as* Compsognathus, *although it was probably an omnivore (eating anything, plant or animal matter).*

- **The four middle teeth** of *Heterodontosaurus* were long and curved, similar to the tusks of a wild boar, and may have been used to fight rivals or in self-defence.

- **The back teeth** were long and had sharp tops, or cusps, for chewing.

Pegomastax

- *Pegomastax*, which means 'thick or strong jaw', dates back to 200–190 mya and has some extremely unusual features.

- **It belonged to the *Heterodontosaurus* group**, with most members having different-shaped teeth, with two or four enlarged as long, fang-like canines.

- **In *Pegomastax***, these fangs in the lower jaw were relatively long, giving a vampire-like appearance.

- *Pegomastax* **also had** a parrot-like horny beak at the front of its mouth for pecking and slicing.

- **Another strange feature** was a covering of long bristles that have been likened to those of a porcupine.

- **The long teeth may have been used** to rip fruit, stab small animal victims, slash at enemies, display open-mouthed to rivals, or even dig for food.

- *Pegomastax* **was very small**, hardly more than 60 cm long.

- **Its fossils come from Early Jurassic rocks** in South Africa and were first excavated in the 1960s, but not named until recently, in 2012.

▲ The tough body bristles of Pegomastax may have worked as protection, not only from enemies, but while scurrying through thick, thorny undergrowth.

DID YOU KNOW?

For almost 50 years the fossils of Pegomastax remained in cupboards and drawers at Harvard University, USA, waiting to be studied.

Fruitadens

- *Fruitadens* **is named** not after a fruit-eating diet, but the place where its fossils were dug up, Fruita in Colorado, USA.

- **Living about 150–145 mya**, in the Late Jurassic Period, *Fruitadens* was one of the last of the small dinosaur group known as heterodontosaurs.

- **Fossil parts** of about four or possibly five individuals are known, together representing jaws, backbones and some front and rear limb bones.

- **These fossils were collected** from the 1970s but only assembled and described in 2010.

- **Like other heterodontosaurs**, *Fruitadens* had two longer teeth called canines, one on either side near the front of the lower jaw.

- *Fruitadens* **was very small** and lightly built, less than 80 cm long and weighing less than one kilogram.

- **It had long but well-muscled legs** and probably relied on speed and agility for survival.

- *Fruitadens* **would dart on its back legs** into the undergrowth or among rocks to escape from predators.

- *Fruitadens* **was probably an omnivore**, eating any small items such as leaves, seeds, tubers, insects, eggs and worms.

▶ Fruitadens *was one of the smallest of all known non-bird dinosaurs.*

Iguanodon

- **Part of the ornithopod group**, *Iguanodon* was a large plant-eating dinosaur. It lived during the Early to Middle Cretaceous Period, 130–125 mya.

- **Numerous fossils** of *Iguanodon* have been found in several countries in Europe, especially Belgium, with similar fossils from England, Germany and Spain.

- *Iguanodon* **measured** about 10–11 m from nose to tail. It probably weighed 4–5 tonnes, about the size of an elephant.

- *Iguanodon* **probably walked** and ran on its large, powerful back legs for much of the time, with its body held horizontal.

- **A cone-shaped spike** on the thumb may have been used as a weapon for jabbing at rivals or enemies.

- **The three central fingers** on the hands had hoof-like claws for occasional four-legged walking.

- **The fifth**, or little finger, was able to bend across the hand for grasping objects, and was perhaps used to pull plants towards the mouth.

DID YOU KNOW?

Iguanodon was one of the very first dinosaurs to be given an official scientific name in 1825.

◀ Iguanodon *is well known from the fossils of many individuals.*

Brachylophosaurus

- **Brachylophosaurus was a hadrosaur** or duckbill that lived in what are now Alberta, Canada, and Montana, USA, in North America.

- **With a length of around 9 m**, and a weight of 2–3 tonnes, *Brachylophosaurus* was average size for the hadrosaur group.

- **Its bony head crest** was not upright, but like a shield or plate lying flat on the top of the forehead region, behind the eyes.

- **The head crest of *Brachylophosaurus*** does not seem to be strong enough for headbutting rivals or enemies. It may have been a visual sign of adulthood, maturity and readiness to breed.

- **The toothless front of the mouth** of *Brachylophosaurus* was wide and flat, and one of the most 'duck-bill-like' of the duckbills.

- **The rear of the mouth** had hundreds of teeth arranged in ranks called batteries, for powerful thorough chewing of tough plant food.

- **In life**, the cheeks were probably fleshy pouches that kept the food in the mouth while it was chewed.

- **Brachylophosaurus lived** towards the end of the Age of Dinosaurs, some 76–75 mya.

- **One of the best-preserved dinosaurs** ever found was a *Brachylophosaurus* nicknamed 'Elvis'.

> **DID YOU KNOW?**
> Nicknames for well preserved specimens of Brachylophosaurus, as well as 'Elvis', include 'Leonardo', 'Roberta', 'Peanut' and Marco'.

▲ *The ranks or batteries of chewing cheek teeth are clearly visible in this skull of Brachylophosaurus.*

Latirhinus

- **Latirhinus is one** of the most recently discovered hadrosaurs, named in 2012.

- **Its fossils are from** the Late Cretaceous Period, 80–70 mya, when many kinds of hadrosaurs were evolving.

- **The remains of *Latirhinus*** were dug from the Cerro del Pueblo Formation in Coahuila, Northern Mexico.

- **These rocks have also yielded fossils** of other hadrosaurs, horned dinosaurs (ceratopsians), pterosaurs and turtles.

- **Latirhinus** is one of the most southern of all hadrosaurs, most of which came from northern lands.

- **One of its main features** was its extra-large nose or snout, making up almost half of the head's length.

- **The name *Latirhinus*** means 'wide or broad nose'.

- **This very large nose** could have had a flap of loose skin that was blown up like a balloon, to make sounds or for visual display.

- **From similar hadrosaurs**, the size of *Latirhinus* was about 9 m long and 3 tonnes in weight.

▲ Latirhinus *may have used its nose flap to make honking sounds or to inflate like a balloon and attract mates at breeding time.*

Feeding and digestion

The teeth and digestive systems of dinosaurs were specialized for the food that they ate. Plants are more difficult to digest than meat, so dinosaurs that ate plants had more complex digestive systems than meat-eaters. These systems tended to be fairly large and heavy, so plant-eating dinosaurs had bigger bodies and tended to move more slowly.

COPROLITES

Fossilized droppings are called coprolites. The size and shape of dinosaur coprolites can reveal much about the digestive system they have come from, while fossilized contents can show what the dinosaur had eaten.

► *BEAK MOUTH*
The front mouths of most ornithischian dinosaurs, such as this Lambeosaurus, had a horny covering rather like a bird's beak. These were different shapes and sizes depending on the food gathered.

Some dinosaurs relied on tough teeth and strong jaw muscles to grind up food before it was swallowed. These teeth were usually wide and flat with ridges or grinding surfaces. Others had simple teeth that did not chew the food, but they had complex digestive systems to break food down once it had been swallowed. Plant-eaters were in turn eaten by meat-eating dinosaurs. These creatures had smaller and simpler digestive systems as meat is easier to digest. This allowed them to have lighter bodies and to move more quickly, which helped them hunt prey. Meat-eaters had sharp, pointed teeth to kill their prey and tear off chunks of flesh.

▲ *PLANT-EATING HADROSAURS*
Among the most successful plant-eating dinosaurs were the hadrosaurs. They browsed on leaves from forests and bushes, eating twigs and shoots as well as leaves.

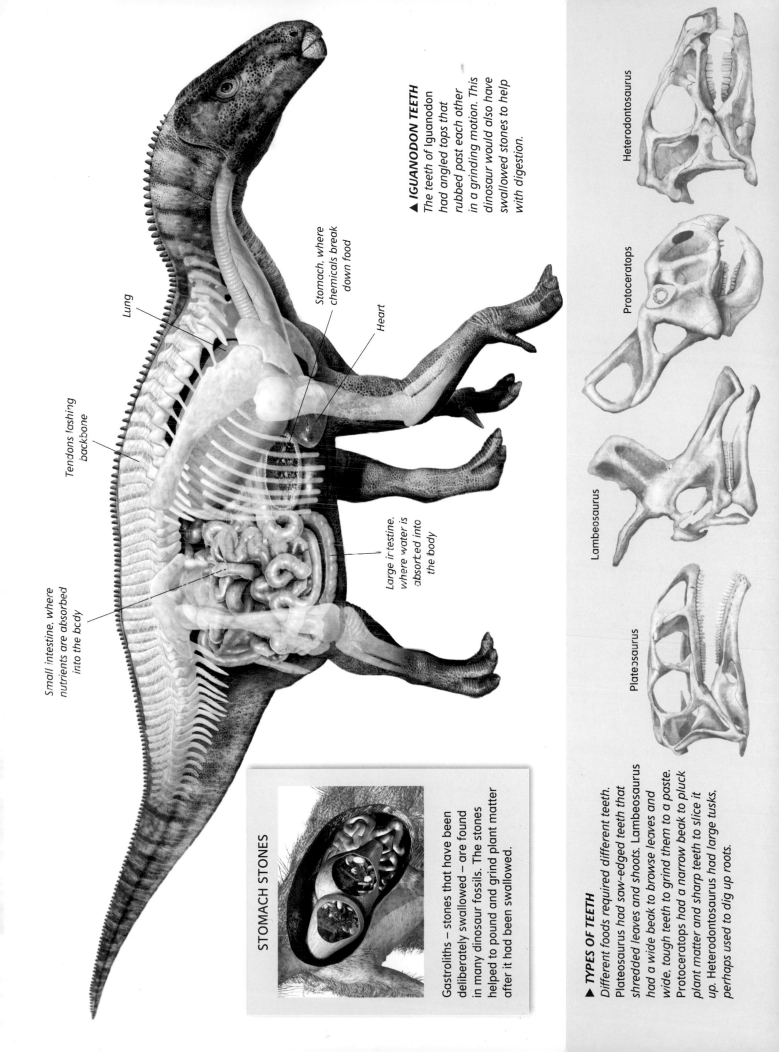

Lung

Tendons lashing backbone

Small intestine, where nutrients are absorbed into the body

Stomach, where chemicals break down food

Heart

Large intestine, where water is absorbed into the body

▲ **IGUANODON TEETH**
The teeth of Iguanodon had angled tops that rubbed past each other in a grinding motion. This dinosaur would also have swallowed stones to help with digestion.

Heterodontosaurus

Protoceratops

Lambeosaurus

Plateosaurus

STOMACH STONES

Gastroliths – stones that have been deliberately swallowed – are found in many dinosaur fossils. The stones helped to pound and grind plant matter after it had been swallowed.

▶ **TYPES OF TEETH**
Different foods required different teeth. Plateosaurus had saw-edged teeth that shredded leaves and shoots. Lambeosaurus had a wide beak to browse leaves and wide, tough teeth to grind them to a paste. Protoceratops had a narrow beak to pluck plant matter and sharp teeth to slice it up. Heterodontosaurus had large tusks, perhaps used to dig up roots.

Psittacosaurus

● **Psittacosaurus was a plant-eater**, and an early relative of the group known as ceratopsians, or 'horn-faced' dinosaurs.

● **Appearing in the Middle Cretaceous Period**, different species of *Psittacosaurus* lived from 125–100 mya.

● **Psittacosaurus was named** in 1923 from fossils found in Mongolia, in Central Asia. Fossils have been found at various sites across Asia, including Russia, China and Thailand.

● **The rear legs** of *Psittacosaurus* were longer and stronger than its front legs, suggesting that this dinosaur may have reared up to run fast on its rear legs, rather than running on all four legs.

▶ *In one fossil discovery, an adult* Psittacosaurus *was found with more than 30 young, which it may have been looking after.*

● **Psittacosaurus measured** about 2 m long, weighed around 20 kg and had four toes on each foot.

● **The name *Psittacosaurus*** means 'parrot reptile', after the dinosaur's beak-shaped mouth, similar to that of a parrot.

● **Inside its cheeks**, *Psittacosaurus* had many sharp teeth capable of cutting and slicing through tough plant material.

DID YOU KNOW?

Fossil evidence shows that when newly hatched from their eggs, baby Psittacosaurus were hardly longer than a human hand.

Protoceratops

● **Protoceratops was an early kind** of horned dinosaur or ceratopsian, living some 77–70 mya.

● **It has some features** of its ancestors, and also some of later ceratopsians, such as a neck frill or shield.

● **However the nose horn** of *Protoceratops* was hardly developed, unlike other ceratopsians.

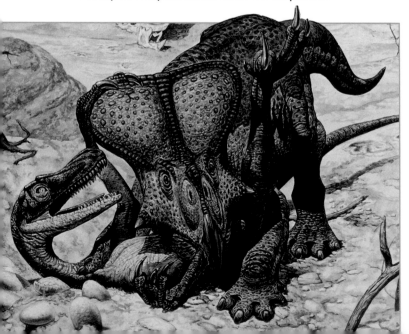

● **The neck frill was not solid** but had gaps or 'windows' probably to save weight, which in life would have been filled in with skin.

● **Protoceratops was about the size of a pig**, around 1.8 m long and weighed 150 kg.

● **Lots of fossils** found near each other suggest *Protoceratops* lived and travelled in herds.

● **Remains of *Protoceratops*** come from east Asia, especially Mongolia.

● **They were first dug out** in 1922 by a group of American palaeontologists and adventurers who were hoping to find fossils of early humans or 'ape-men'.

● **One find of dinosaur nests and eggs** – the first ever to be identified – was said to have been laid by *Protoceratops*.

● **However later studies showed** they belonged to the beaked theropod *Oviraptor*.

◀ *One fossil find shows how* Protoceratops *(right) may have battled with the meat-eater* Velociraptor *(left).*

Spinops

- **Spinops** is one of the latest ceratopsians, or horned dinosaurs, to receive a name, in 2011.

- **It is also** one of the dinosaurs with the longest time span between its fossils being collected and their official description and naming – almost 100 years.

- **The remains were collected** in Alberta, Canada in 1916, from the well-known Red Deer River 'bonebed' rocks.

- **The collectors** were the famous Sternberg family, who were led by father Charles H Sternberg.

- **They sent the fossils** to London's Natural History Museum, and two years later received a letter saying the remains were 'nothing but rubbish'.

- **Mainly parts of the skull** of *Spinops* were found, but they are enough for it to be identified, through recent study, as a new kind of ceratopsian.

- **The Sternbergs dug up fossils** of dozens of kinds of dinosaurs, fish and other prehistoric creatures.

▼ The full name of this ceratopsian is Spinops sternbergorum, in honour of the Sternberg family.

- **Using information** from similar but more complete finds, *Spinops* is estimated at about 6 m long and weighing 1–2 tonnes.

- **On each side of *Spinops'* frill** was one long slightly curved horn pointing up and back, and one smaller, curved, hook-shaped horn facing forwards and down.

Ajkaceratops

▼ Ajkaceratops probably used its beak to snip off low vegetation, which was chewed by its batteries of cheek teeth.

- **Ajkaceratops was one** of the smallest ceratopsians or horned dinosaurs, probably less than one metre long.

- **Its fossils were discovered** near Ajka, Hungary, leading to the name 'horn-face of Ajka', given in 2010.

- **This discovery** extended the known range of ceratopsians from North America and Asia into Europe.

- **The toothless**, beak-shaped front of the mouth is usually recognized as typical for a ceratopsian.

- **But in the case of *Ajkaceratops***, the curved bone forming part of the lower jaw was first identified as a toe bone of a hoofed mammal.

- **On turning the bone around**, palaeontologists saw it came from the jaw of a small horn-faced dinosaur.

- **The fossils** were found in a bauxite (aluminium ore) mine in the Bakony Mountains near Ajka, in 2009.

- **The remains are from 85 mya**, when parts of Europe were flooded, forming a series of large islands.

- **As sea levels rose** and fell, it appears that ceratopsian dinosaurs and other animals 'island-hopped' from Asia and evolved into new types.

DID YOU KNOW?

Fossils found with those of Ajkaceratops include those of meat-eating dinosaurs, crocodiles, pterosaurs, birds, lizards, turtles and fish.

Xenoceratops

- **Officially named in 2012**, the fossils of *Xenoceratops* or 'strange horn face' were originally dug up in 1958.

- **The fossils of *Xenoceratops*** come from Alberta, Canada, and are about 80–75 million years old.

- **These are the oldest remains** of any horn-faced, or ceratopsian dinosaur, found in Canada.

- ***Xenoceratops* was a fairly standard size** for a ceratopsian, at about 6 m long and scaling some 2 tonnes.

- **Even though it was quite early** in the evolution of large ceratopsians, *Xenoceratops* already had a large neck frill with horns and bumps.

- **In particular it had two long**, stout, spike-like horns on either side at the top of the frill, pointing up and slightly outwards.

- **There may have also been** smaller, cone-shaped lumps further down the edge of the frill.

- **Experts studying the fossils** recently realized they had never been officially described or named, and that they represented a new kind of ceratopsian.

- **Experts then discovered** a 'field jacket', a plaster casing containing fossils to protect them during excavation and transport, which was over 50 years old.

- **The jacket contained** more remains identified as belonging to *Xenoceratops*.

▶ *The exact position of the front horns of Xenoceratops, plus the bony mound or 'boss' in front of them, are not certain.*

Triceratops

- **Many fossil remains** of *Triceratops* have been found. It is one of the most-studied and best known dinosaurs, and lived at the very end of the Age of Dinosaurs, 68–66 mya.

- ***Triceratops* was the largest** of the plant-eating ceratopsians, or 'horn-faced' dinosaurs.

- **Fossils of more than** 100 *Triceratops* have been discovered in North America, though no truly complete skeletons.

- ***Triceratops* was about 9 m** long and weighed up to 10 tonnes – as big as the largest elephants of today.

- **As well as a short nose horn** and two one-metre eyebrow horns, *Triceratops* also had a wide, sweeping frill that covered its neck like a curved plate.

- **The neck frill** may have been an anchor for the dinosaur's powerful chewing muscles.

- **Acting as a shield**, the bony neck frill may have protected *Triceratops* as it faced predators head-on.

▲ *The beak, head and neck frill of* Triceratops *made up almost a quarter of its length.*

- **The neck frill** may also have been brightly coloured to impress rivals or enemies – or even potential mates.

- **The beak-like front** of *Triceratops'* mouth was toothless, but its cheeks contained sharp teeth for chewing plants.

Pachycephalosaurs

Extra thick skull bone

- **One of the last** dinosaur groups to appear were the pachycephalosaurs. Most lived 80–66 mya.

- **They are named after** one of the best known members of the group, *Pachycephalosaurus*.

- ***Pachycephalosaurus*** means 'thick-headed reptile', due to the domed and hugely thickened bone on the top of its skull – like a cyclist's crash helmet.

- **About 4.5 m long** from nose to tail, *Pachycephalosaurus* lived in the American Midwest.

- ***Stegoceras***, also from the American Midwest, was about 2 m long with a body the size of a goat.

- ***Homalocephale***, about 2 m long, lived in Asia 80 mya. It had a flatter skull, but some experts think it was a young *Prenocephale*.

- **Pachycephalosaurs** may have defended themselves by lowering their heads and charging at enemies.

- **At breeding time**, the males may have tried to butt each other, but how and where is not clear.

▲ *Typical of its group, Pachycephalosaurus had a thickened layer of bone on the top of its head.*

DID YOU KNOW?

Pachycephalosaurs are often known as the 'bone-heads', 'dome-heads', or 'helmet-heads'.

Prenocephale

- ***Prenocephale* was one of the last** of the 'bone-heads' or pachycephalosaur dinosaurs, and indeed one of the last of all dinosaurs, living around 70 or less mya.

- **It was quite small**, around 1.8–2.5 m long and between 80–140 kg in weight.

- **The size of *Prenocephale*** is vague because it is estimated, as limited numbers of its fossils have been found in East Asia.

- **However there are enough** *Prenocephale* remains to show it was similar in body shape to other, better-known bone-heads.

- ***Prenocephale* had a thickened**, egg-shaped upper skull, like a smooth dome.

- **Around the lower edges of the dome**, like the brim of a hat stretching down to the front of the snout, were a row of small lumps, bumps and spikes.

- **The eyes of *Prenocephale*** were large and faced partly forwards to see in detail and judge distances.

- **The eating habits of *Prenocephale***, and most pachycephalosaurs, are not clear. Most experts think they ate soft plant material, with perhaps small worms and bugs and eggs, but their teeth were small and not very strong.

- **Fossils of *Prenocephale*** were discovered during an expedition by Polish, Mongolian and Russian fossil experts to the Gobi Desert.

◀ *A herd of Prenocephale scatters in panic as it is attacked by the giant carnivore Tarbosaurus (which may be the Asian form of Tyrannosaurus).*

Beaks

● **Several kinds of dinosaurs** had a toothless, beak-shaped front to their mouths.

● **Beaked dinosaurs** included ceratopsians (horn-faces) such as *Triceratops*, ornithopods such as *Iguanodon* and the hadrosaurs (duckbills), stegosaurs, ankylosaurs (armoured dinosaurs) and fast-running ostrich dinosaurs.

● **Most beaked dinosaurs** had chopping or chewing teeth near the backs of their mouths or in their cheeks, but ostrich dinosaurs had no teeth.

● **A dinosaur's beak** was made up of the upper (maxilla) and the lower (dentary or mandible) jaw bones.

● **The bones at the front** of a dinosaur's jaw would have been covered with horn, which formed the outer shape of the beak.

● **Dinosaurs almost certainly used** their beaks for pecking, snipping, tearing and slicing their food. They may also have used their beaks to peck fiercely at attackers.

▶ Protoceratops *had a tall skull with deep jaws tipped by a sharp beak.*

▼ Muttaburrasaurus *may have been an early member of the dinosaur group known as the ceratopsians or 'horn-faces'. It had the characteristic bird-like beak, but had not yet evolved the face horns or neck shield.*

DID YOU KNOW?

Some of the largest beaks in relation to body size belonged to Oviraptor and Psittacosaurus.

Teeth

● **Some of the most common** fossil remains are of dinosaur teeth – the hardest parts of their bodies.

● **Dinosaur teeth** come in a huge range of sizes and shapes – daggers, knives, shears, pegs, combs, rakes, file-like rasps, crushing batteries and vices.

● **In some dinosaurs**, up to three quarters of a tooth was fixed into the jaw bone, so only one quarter was actually visible.

● **The teeth of plant-eaters** such as *Iguanodon* had angled tops that rubbed past each other in a grinding motion.

● **Some duckbill dinosaurs** (hadrosaurs) had more than 1000 teeth, all at the back of the mouth.

▼ Edmontosaurus *had no front teeth, only a flattened 'duck-bill'.*

Batteries of teeth for crushing plants

◀ Tyrannosaurus *had 50-plus 'banana' teeth. They were long and strong for tearing flesh and crushing bone.*

● **Like modern reptiles**, dinosaurs probably grew new teeth to replace old, worn or broken ones.

● **Some of the largest teeth** of any dinosaur belonged to 9-m-long *Daspletosaurus*, a tyrannosaur-like meat-eater. They measured up to 18 cm in length.

Eyes

- **No fossils have been found** of dinosaur eyes because they were made of soft tissue that soon rotted away after death, or they were eaten by scavengers.

- **The main clues** to dinosaur eyes come from the bowl-like hollows, or orbits, in the skull where the eyes were located.

- **The orbits** in fossil skulls show that dinosaur eyes were similar to those of reptiles today.

- **The 6-m-long sauropod** *Vulcanodon* had tiny eyes relative to the size of its head.

- **Small-eyed dinosaurs** probably only had good vision in the daytime.

- **Many plant-eating dinosaurs** had eyes on the sides of their heads, giving all-round vision.

- **The small meat-eater** *Troodon* had relatively large eyes, and it could probably see well, even in dim light.

- *Troodon's* **eyes** were on the front of its head pointing forwards, allowing it to see detail and judge distance.

- **Dinosaurs that had large bulges**, called optic lobes, in their brains – detectable by the shapes of their skulls – could probably see well, perhaps even at night.

◀ Tyrannosaurus rex *had eyes that were set at an angle so they looked more to the front than to the sides. This allowed* T rex *to see an object in front with both eyes and judge its distance well.*

DID YOU KNOW?
The plant-eater *Leaellynasaura* had large optic lobes, and probably had good eyesight.

Brains

- **There is a broad link** between the size of an animal's brain compared to the size of its body, and the level of intelligence it shows.

- **Some fossil dinosaur skulls** have preserved the hollow where the brain once was, revealing its approximate size and shape.

- **In some cases**, a lump of rock formed inside a fossil skull, taking on the size and shape of the brain.

▼ *Small meat-eaters such as* Troodon *had the biggest brains for their body size, and probably showed the most intelligence.*

▶ Camarasaurus *had one of the smallest brains for its body size of any dinosaur – about the size of a human fist.*

- **The tiny brain** of *Stegosaurus* weighed about 70–80 g, while the whole dinosaur weighed perhaps 4 tonnes.

- **The brain** of *Stegosaurus* was only 1/50,000th of the weight of its whole body (in a human it is 1/50th).

- *Brachiosaurus'* **brain** was perhaps only 1/100,000th of the weight of its whole body.

- **The brain of the small meat-eater** *Troodon* was about 1/100th the weight of its body, which means that *Troodon* was probably one of the most intelligent dinosaurs.

- **The brain-body size comparison** for most dinosaurs is much the same as that of living reptiles.

- **Small- and medium-sized** meat-eaters such as *Troodon* may have been as intelligent as parrots or rats.

- **It was once thought** that *Stegosaurus* had a 'second brain' in the base of its tail. This lump is now thought to have been a nerve junction.

Eggs and nests

Dinosaurs laid eggs in which their young developed before hatching. The eggs were similar to those of modern birds. They had hard shells through which oxygen could reach the young, but which gave protection against predators and drying out. Membranes inside separated the parts of the egg – food in the yolk, water in the albumen and the growing animal.

Scientists have found many dinosaur nests. Some of these were very simple, consisting of eggs laid in a circle or a row. Others were complex with layers of vegetation, sand or mud carefully arranged to protect the eggs. Eggs need to be kept warm, so they might have been buried in warm sand or covered with leaves that heat up as they rot away.

Some dinosaur parents stayed with the nest and cared for their young. Others ignored the eggs once they had been laid. The young had to look after themselves as soon as they hatched.

LAYING EGGS

Sauropods dug round bowls in soft earth to act as nests, then squatted to lay their eggs. There may have been 12–15 eggs in each nest, but it is not clear if the sauropod covered the eggs over.

▶ *BRINGING FOOD*
Maiasaura parents brought leaves to the nest to feed their young. This gave the young a better chance of survival.

▲ *GOOD MOTHER*
Maiasaura, which means 'Good Mother Lizard' was named because scientists found its nests in colonies, consisting of eggs, embryos and juveniles.

▼ *EGG STAGES*
The developing young were protected by their eggs and nourished by the yolk inside.
1 *Tiny embryo nourished by yolk*
2 *Developing embryo*
3 *Fully formed baby fills the space inside egg*
4 *Hatchling*

▼ *JUST HATCHED*
When Maiasaura young first hatched they were unable to walk as their legs were not fully formed. They fed on food brought by the adults until they were about one year old.

Chorion membrane

Amniotic sac

▼ *GROWING UP*
After they left the nest, the young Maiasaura may have stayed with their parents for several more years. The parents would have guarded the young and may have shown them what was good to eat.

▼ *BURROWING DEEP*
Oryctodromeus was a small burrowing dinosaur that lived 95 million years ago. It dug underground burrows in which to lay its eggs and raise its young.

Sails

● **Long, bony extensions**, like rods or spines, stuck up from the backs of some dinosaurs.

● **These extensions** may have held up a large area of skin, commonly called a back sail.

● **Dinosaurs with back sails** included the meat-eater *Spinosaurus* and the plant-eater *Ouranosaurus*.

● *Spinosaurus* and *Ouranosaurus* both lived more than 100 mya.

● **Fossils of *Spinosaurus*** and *Ouranosaurus* were found in North Africa.

● **The skin on a back sail** may have been brightly coloured, or may even have changed colour, like the skin of a chameleon lizard today.

● **Colours and patterns** could have been used to startle enemies, deter rivals, and impress mates at breeding time.

● **A back sail** may have helped to control body temperature. Standing sideways to the sun, it would absorb the sun's heat and allow the dinosaur to warm up quickly.

● **Standing in the shade**, a back sail would lose warmth and help the dinosaur avoid overheating.

▲ *Blood vessels spread over bony rods in the sail of* Spinosaurus *may have helped to carry away heat and regulate body temperature.*

Horns

● **A dinosaur's horns got bigger** as the animal grew. Each horn had a bony core and an outer covering of a tough material formed mainly from keratin – the same substance that makes up human hair and fingernails.

● **Horns were most common** among plant-eating dinosaurs. They were probably used for defence and to protect young against predators.

● **The biggest horns** belonged to the ceratopsians or 'horn-faces', such as *Triceratops*.

● **In some ceratopsian horns**, the bony core alone was about one metre long. This did not include the outer sheath, so the whole horn would have been longer.

● **The ceratopsian *Styracosaurus***, or 'spiked reptile', had a series of long horns around the top of its neck frill, and a very long horn on its nose.

● **Horns may have been used** in head-swinging displays to intimidate rivals and make physical fighting less likely.

DID YOU KNOW?

Dinosaurs may have used their horns to push over plants or dig up roots for food.

▲ *If an enemy came near,* Styracosaurus *may have charged with its head down, and jabbed with its long, sharp horn. The wide frill of bone over its neck made it look even more scary.*

● **In battle**, male dinosaurs may have locked horns in a trial of strength, as antelopes do today.

● **Armoured dinosaurs** such as the nodosaur *Panoplosaurus* had horn-like spikes along the sides of the body, especially in the shoulder region.

Noses

● **Dinosaurs breathed** through their mouths and/or noses, just like many other creatures do today.

● **Fossil dinosaur skulls** show that there were two nose openings, called nares, in the bone.

● **The nasal openings**, or nares, led to nasal chambers inside the skull, where the smell organs were located.

● **Some meat-eaters**, especially carnosaurs such as *Allosaurus* and *Tyrannosaurus*, had very large nasal chambers and probably had an excellent sense of smell.

● **In most dinosaurs**, the nasal openings were at the front of the snout, just above the upper jaw.

● **In some dinosaurs**, especially sauropods such as *Mamenchisaurus* and *Brachiosaurus*, the nasal openings were higher on the skull, between the eyes.

● **Fossils show** that air passages led backwards from the nasal chambers into the head for breathing.

● **The nasal openings** led to external openings, or nostrils, in the skin.

Nares

▲ *The nares (nasal openings) at the snout tip of* Tyrannosaurus *were especially large.*

DID YOU KNOW?

In hadrosaurs, the nasal passages inside the bony head crests were more than one metre long.

● **New evidence from modern animals** suggests that a dinosaur's nostrils would have been lower down than the nares, towards the front of the snout.

Speed

● **The fastest dinosaurs** had long, slim, muscular legs and small, lightweight bodies.

● **Ostrich dinosaurs** were probably the speediest, perhaps attaining the same top speed as today's ostrich – 70 km/h.

● **The main leg muscles** of the ostrich dinosaur *Struthiomimus* were in its hips and thighs.

● **The hip and leg design** of ostrich dinosaurs meant they could swing their limbs to and fro quickly, like those of a modern racehorse.

● **Large, powerful, plant-eating dinosaurs**, such as the duckbill *Edmontosaurus*, may have pounded along on their huge back legs at 40 km/h.

● **Plant-eaters** such as *Muttaburrasaurus* and *Iguanodon* may have trotted along at 10–12 km/h for several hours.

● **Some experts** once suggested that huge meat-eater *Tyrannosaurus* may have been able to run at 50 km/h.

● **Other experts think** *Tyrannosaurus* was a relatively slow runner at 20 km/h.

● **The slowest dinosaurs** were giant sauropods such as *Brachiosaurus*, which probably plodded at 4–6 km/h (about human walking speed).

● **The fastest land animal today**, the cheetah, would beat any dinosaur with its maximum burst of speed of more than 100 km/h.

▼ *In 2007, computer predictions based on data taken from fossils suggested that the top speed of* Tyrannosaurus *may have been about 28 km/h.*

Colours

● **No one knows** for certain what colours most dinosaurs were.

● **Some fossil specimens** of dinosaur skin show patterns or shading, but all are stone coloured, as fossils are living things that have turned to stone.

● **Recent detailed fossil finds** have allowed the study of microscopic details of structures called melanosomes in dinosaur feathers, that give clues to colours.

● **The feathered dinosaur** *Sinosauropteryx* probably had white and reddish ginger feathers.

● **According to some experts**, certain dinosaurs may have been bright yellow, red or blue, and possibly striped or patched, like some of today's lizards and snakes are.

● **Some dinosaurs** may have been brightly coloured to frighten off predators or to intimidate rivals at breeding time. Colours may have also attracted potential mates.

▼ *The 2-m-long* Dilong *had hair-like feathers, whose tiny structures in well-preserved specimens give some clues to colours. However for the vast majority of reconstructions from fossils, the colours are intelligent guesswork.*

● **Tall 'sails'** on the backs of the plant-eater *Ouranosaurus* and the meat-eater *Spinosaurus* may have been for visual display, as well as for temperature control.

● **The large, bony back plates** on stegosaurs may have been used for colourful displays to rivals and mates.

● **The large neck frills of dinosaurs** such as *Triceratops* may have been colourful and used for display purposes.

● **Some dinosaurs may have been similar** in colour to crocodiles – dull greens and browns, to help camouflage them among trees, rocks and earth.

Armour

● **Many kinds of dinosaurs** had protective 'armour'.

● **Some armour** took the form of bony plates, or osteoderms, embedded in the skin.

● **A dinosaur with armour** might weigh twice as much as a same-sized dinosaur without armour.

● **Armoured dinosaurs** are divided into two main groups – the ankylosaurs and the nodosaurs.

● **The large sauropod** *Saltasaurus*, unusual for its group, had a kind of armour in the form of hundreds of small, bony lumps packed together in the skin of its back.

● **On its back**, *Saltasaurus* also had about 50 larger pieces of bone, each one the size of a human hand.

● *Saltasaurus* **is named** after the Salta region of Argentina, where its fossils were found. Its fossils have also been found in Uruguay, South America.

● *Saltasaurus* **was 12 m long** and weighed about 6–8 tonnes.

▶ *The bony lumps of* Saltasaurus *were scattered over its back and sides.*

Coprolites

● **Coprolites are the fossilized droppings**, or dung, of animals from long ago, such as dinosaurs. Like other fossils, they have become solid rock.

● **Thousands of dinosaur coprolites** have been found at fossil sites across the world.

▲ *Fossilized dinosaur dung may provide clues as to the kind of food eaten by dinosaurs.*

DID YOU KNOW?

One of the largest dinosaur coprolites found measures 44 cm in length and was probably produced by Tyrannosaurus.

● **Cracking or cutting** open coprolites may reveal what the dinosaur had eaten.

● **Coprolites produced** by large meat-eaters such as *Tyrannosaurus* contain bone from their prey.

● **The microscopic structure** of the bones found in coprolites shows the age of the prey when it was eaten. Most victims were very young or old, as these were the easiest creatures for a predator to kill.

● **Coprolites produced** by small meat-eaters such as *Compsognathus* may contain the hard bits of insects, such as the legs and wing cases of beetles.

● **Huge piles** of coprolites found in Montana, USA, were probably produced by the large plant-eater *Maiasaura*.

● ***Maiasaura* coprolites** contain the remains of cones, buds and the needle-like leaves of conifer trees, showing that these dinosaurs had a diet of tough plant matter.

Footprints

● **Fossilized dinosaur footprints** have been found all over the world.

● **Some dinosaurs left footprints** when they walked on the soft mud or sand of riverbanks. Then the mud baked hard in the sun, and was covered by more sand or mud, which helped preserve the footprints as fossils.

● **Some footprints were made** when dinosaur feet left impressions in soft mud or sand that was then covered by volcanic ash, which set hard.

● **Many footprints** have been found together in lines, called 'trackways'. These suggest that some dinosaurs lived in groups, or used the same routes regularly.

● **The distance between** same-sized footprints indicates whether a dinosaur was walking, trotting or running.

● **Footprints of big meat-eaters** such as *Tyrannosaurus* show three toes with claws, on a forward-facing foot.

DID YOU KNOW?

In 2009 sauropod footprints 1.7 m across were found in the Jura region of France.

▲ *Fossilized footprints are called trace fossils because they are signs or prints made by dinosaurs, or other creatures, rather than actual body parts.*

● **In big plant-eaters**, such as *Iguanodon*, each footprint shows three separate toes, but less or no claw impressions, and the feet point slightly inwards.

● **In giant plant-eating sauropods**, each footprint is rounded and has indentations of nail-like 'hooves'.

● **Some sauropod footprints** are more than one metre across.

Herds

- **When fossils of many individuals** of the same dinosaur type are found together, there are various possible causes.

- **One reason is because** their bodies were swept to the same place by a flood, although they may have originally been living in different places.

- **The dinosaurs may have died** in the same place if they had lived there as a group or herd.

- **There is much evidence** that various dinosaur types lived in groups or herds, examples being *Diplodocus*, *Triceratops* and *Iguanodon*.

- **Many fossil footprints** found together heading the same way also suggest that some dinosaurs lived in herds.

- **Some fossil groups** include dinosaurs of different ages, from babies to youngsters and adults.

- **Footprints of a plant-eating dinosaur** have been found with the prints of a meat-eater to one side of them – perhaps evidence of a hunter pursuing its victim.

- **Prints all pointing** in the same direction indicate a herd travelling together to the same place.

- **Sometimes larger footprints** are found to the sides of smaller ones, possibly indicating that adults guarded their young between them.

- **Many jumbled prints** in what was once mud suggests a group of dinosaurs came to drink at a riverbank or lakeside.

◄ *A mixed-age herd would have left similar footprints of different sizes.*

> **DID YOU KNOW?**
> At Peace River Canyon, British Columbia, Canada, some 1700 footprints were found.

Migrations

- **Today, almost no land reptiles** go on regular, long-distance journeys, called migrations.

- **Over the past 30 years**, some scientists have suggested that certain dinosaurs regularly migrated.

- **Evidence for migrating dinosaurs** comes from the positions of the continents at the time. In certain regions, cool winters would have prevented the growth of enough plants for dinosaurs to eat.

- **Fossil evidence suggests** that some plants stopped growing during very hot or dry periods, so some dinosaurs would have migrated to find food.

- **The footprints or tracks** of many dinosaurs travelling in herds is possible evidence that some dinosaurs migrated.

- **Dinosaurs that may have migrated** include *Pachyrhinosaurus*, sauropods such as *Diplodocus* and *Camarasaurus*, and ornithopods such as *Iguanodon* and *Muttaburrasaurus*.

- **One huge fossil site** in Alberta, Canada, contains the fossils of about 1000 *Pachyrhinosaurus* – perhaps a migrating herd that got caught in a flood.

- **In North America**, enormous herds of horned dinosaurs may have migrated north for the brief sub-Arctic summer.

- **In 2012**, teeth from *Camarasaurus* suggested they migrated perhaps 300 km each way to avoid the dry season.

▼ *Fossils of* Pachyrhinosaurus *have been found in parts of Alaska that were inside the Arctic Circle at the end of the Cretaceous Period. It is possible they migrated there from farther south.*

Hibernation

● **Dinosaurs may have gone** into an inactive state called torpor or 'hibernation' during cold periods, as many reptiles do today.

● **The plant-eater** *Leaellynasaura*, found at Dinosaur Cove, Australia, may have become torpid due to the yearly cycle of seasons there.

● **Dinosaur Cove** was nearer the South Pole when dinosaurs lived there, 110–105 mya. At this time, the climate was relatively warm, with no ice at the North or South Poles.

● **Dinosaurs living** at Dinosaur Cove would have had to cope with periods of darkness in winter. They may have become torpid to survive the cold.

● **The eye and brain shapes** of *Leaellynasaura* suggest it had good eyesight, which would have helped it to see in the winter darkness, or in dim forests.

● **Dinosaur fossils** have been found in the Arctic region near the North Pole.

● **Arctic dinosaurs** either became torpid in winter, or migrated south to warmer regions.

◀ *Leaellynasaura may have slept through the cold season, perhaps protected in a burrow. This 3-m dinosaur had a longer tail, in proportion to body size, than almost any other dinosaur.*

Sounds

● **Few reptiles today** make complicated sounds, except for simple hisses, grunts, coughs and roars.

● **Fossils suggest** that dinosaurs made a variety of sounds in several different ways.

● **The bony, hollow head crests** of duckbills (hadrosaurs) may have been used for making sounds.

● **The head crests** of some hadrosaurs contained tubes called respiratory airways, which were used for breathing.

● **Air blown forcefully** through a hadrosaur's head crest passages could have made the whole crest vibrate.

● **A vibrating head crest** may have made a loud sound like a honk, roar or bellow – similar to an elephant trumpeting with its trunk.

● **Fossil skulls** of some hadrosaurs, such as *Edmontosaurus* and *Kritosaurus*, suggest that there was a loose flap of skin, like a floppy bag, between the nostrils and the eyes.

Bony outer layer of crest

Winding air passages

Skull bone

Outer skin

▶ *Inside the mostly hollow head crest of the hadrosaur Lambeosaurus, the airways or nasal passages followed a winding route.*

● *Kritosaurus* **may have inflated** its loose nasal flap of skin like a balloon to make a honking or bellowing sound, as some seals do today.

Fossil clues

Everything we know about dinosaurs has been learnt from fossils – the remains and traces of these animals found in ancient rocks. Fossils are formed in many ways, and they help us to understand what kinds of animals and plants were living in prehistoric times. Usually, hard parts of an animal, such as the bones, are fossilized most easily. Only rarely do softer body parts become fossils.

Most fossils are partial, where only a part of the dead animal or plant has been preserved. Scientists have to study the parts they have to try to work out what the rest of the animal looked like. For instance, the only fossil of the dinosaur *Yaverlandia* from the Isle of Wight, UK, consists of just half a skull.

◄ OVIRAPTOR, GOBI DESERT
This small feathered dinosaur lived about 75 million years ago and was about 2 m long.

▼ MICRORAPTOR, CHINA
Named for its tiny 50 cm size, this hunter lived about 120 million years ago and had large, wing-like feathers on all four legs.

► REBBACHISAURUS, AFRICA
This sauropod lived in Africa about 100 million years and grew to be about 20 m long. It had a ridge running along its back.

▼ CAMARASAURUS, NORTH AMERICA
This plant-eating sauropod was about 15 m long and lived about 150 million years ago.

▲ MUSSAURUS, SOUTH AMERICA
The name of this dinosaur means 'mouse-lizard' and refers to the small 20 cm size of some 210 million year old fossilized babies that were found.

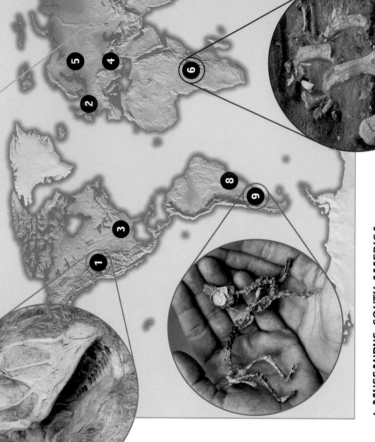

KEY

1	Camarasaurus *North America*	6	Rebbachisaurus *Africa*
2	Megalosaurus *United Kingdom*	7	Oviraptor *Gobi Desert, Asia*
3	Hypsibema *North America*	8	Argentinosaurus *South America*
4	Balaur *Southern Europe*	9	Mussaurus *South America*
5	Plateosaurus *Northern Europe*	10	Microraptor *China*

▶ FOSSIL FORMATION

The stages by which a dinosaur is fossilized.

1 Dinosaur dies and soft body parts rot away
2 Bones become buried under sand, mud or silt
3 Bones are trapped in forming rock for millions of years and become fossilized
4 The rocks are worn away, revealing the fossils

① ② ④

▼ RECONSTRUCTION

This reconstruction of Gryposaurus shows the fossil bones with some external detail such as skin and beak added, as well as internal organs and muscle. Scientists study other fossils and use intelligent guess work to do this.

Beak

Skin

Heart

Lung

Stomach

Tendons

Powerful leg muscles

Intestines

Strong muscles to move tail

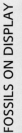

FOSSILS ON DISPLAY

Museums display their best fossils to the public to show what scientists have found and how they learn about prehistoric life. When a fossil is put together as it would have been in life, it shows the size and shape of the once living animal.

Europe

- **The first dinosaur fossils** ever discovered and given official names were found in England in the 1820s.

- **One of the first** almost complete dinosaur skeletons found was that of the big plant-eater *Iguanodon*, in 1871, in southern England.

- **Some of the most numerous** early fossils found were those of *Iguanodon*, discovered in the Belgian village of Bernissart in 1878.

- **About 155–145 mya**, Solnhofen in southern Germany was a mosaic of lush islands and shallow lagoons – ideal for many kinds of life.

- **At Solnhofen**, amazingly detailed fossils of tiny *Compsognathus* and the first-known bird *Archaeopteryx* have been found preserved in sandstone.

- **Fossils of *Compsognathus*** were also found near Nice in southern France.

- **Many fossils** of *Plateosaurus* were recovered from Trossingen, Germany, in 1911–12, 1921–23 and 1932.

- **Some of the largest fossil eggs**, measuring 30 cm long, were thought to have been laid by *Hypselosaurus* near Aix-en-Provence in southern France.

▲ *The dots indicate just a few of the dinosaur fossil sites that are found in Europe.*

- **The Isle of Wight** off southern England has provided so many dinosaur fossils that it is sometimes known as 'Dinosaur Island'.

- **Fossils of *Hypsilophodon*** have been found in eastern Spain, and those of *Camptosaurus* on the coast of Portugal.

Africa

- **The first major discoveries** of African dinosaur fossils were made in 1907 at Tendaguru, present-day Tanzania. They include *Giraffatitan*, *Dicraeosaurus*, and *Kentrosaurus*.

- **Remains of *Cetiosaurus*** were found in Morocco, north Africa.

- ***Nigersaurus***, a 9-m-long, 10-tonne plant-eater, is known from fossils found in Niger.

- **Fossils of *Spinosaurus*,** the largest meat-eating dinosaur, come from Morocco and Egypt.

- ***Ouranosaurus*** is known from fossils found in Niger.

- **Sauropod fossils** were also found, including *Tornieri* in Tanzania, and *Vulcanodon* in Zimbabwe.

- **Remains of *Massospondylus*,** a plant-eating prosauropod, were found at sites in southern Africa.

- **Fossils named as *Gyposaurus*** have been found in Orange Free State, South Africa.

- **During the 1908–12** expedition to Tendaguru, more than 250 tonnes of fossil bones and rocks were taken 65 km to the nearest port, for transport to Germany.

▼ *In Africa, as elsewhere, fossils are easier to find in places with bare, rocky soils, such as the Sahara region.*

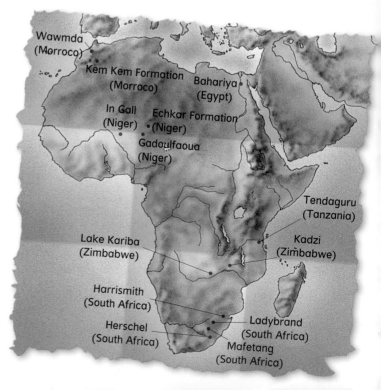

Asia

- **Hundreds of kinds** of dinosaurs have been discovered in Asia.

- **Most Asian dinosaur fossils** found so far are from the Gobi Desert in Central Asia, and in present-day China. Some were also found in present-day India.

- **Remains of *Titanosaurus***, a huge plant-eating sauropod, were uncovered near Umrer, in India. It lived about 70 mya, and was similar in shape to its cousin of the same time, *Saltasaurus*, from South America.

- ***Titanosaurus*** was about 12 m long and weighed 10–15 tonnes.

- **Fossils of the sauropod *Barapasaurus*** were found in India and described and named in 1975.

- ***Barapasaurus*** **was 14 m long** and probably weighed over 10 tonnes. It is one of the first known sauropods, living around 190–180 mya.

- **Fossils of *Dravidosaurus***, once thought to belong to the stegosaur group, were found near Tiruchirapalli in southern India. Further studies suggest they are actually from a type of sea reptile.

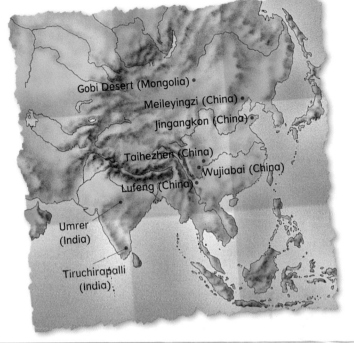

▶ The fossils of Saltasaurus *(shown here)* and Titanosaurus *are very similar, and some experts consider them to be the same type of dinosaur.*

▼ *Dinosaur fossil finds span the vast continent of Asia. (See later pages for more Gobi and China finds.)*

Gobi Desert (Mongolia) •
Meileyingzi (China) •
Jingangkon (China) •
Taihezhen (China) •
• Wujiabai (China)
Lufeng (China) •
Umrer (India) •
Tiruchirapalli (India) •

Gobi Desert

- **The Gobi Desert** covers much of southern Mongolia and parts of northern China.

- **The first fossil-hunting expeditions** to the Gobi Desert took place in 1922–25, and were organized by the American Museum of Natural History.

- **The expeditions** set out to look for fossils of early humans, but instead found amazing dinosaur remains.

- **The first fossil dinosaur eggs** were found by the 1922–25 expeditions.

- ***Velociraptor***, *Avimimus* and *Pinacosaurus* were discovered in the Gobi.

- **Russian expeditions** in 1946 and 1948–49 discovered new armoured and duckbilled dinosaurs.

- **More expeditions** in the 1960s–70s found the sauropod *Opisthocoelicaudia* and the helmet-headed *Prenocephale*.

- **Other Gobi dinosaurs** include *Gallimimus* and *Oviraptor*. In the 1990s–2000s more expeditions uncovered therizinosaurs.

▶ *The Gobi's fossil sites are far from any towns or cities. Searching for fossils is hard work in extreme temperatures and dust storms.*

▶ Gallimimus *fossils were found in the early 1970s in the Nemegt region of the Gobi, which has yielded many exciting remains. There are parts of skeletons of many individuals, ranging from youngsters to adults.*

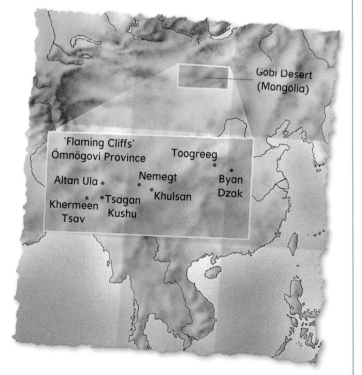

Gobi Desert (Mongolia)

'Flaming Cliffs'
Ömnögovi Province
Toogreeg
Altan Ula •
Nemegt
Byan Dzak
Khermeen Tsav
• Tsagan Kushu
• Khulsan

China

- **For centuries**, dinosaur fossils in China were identified as belonging to mythical creatures such as dragons.

- **The first fossils** studied scientifically in China were uncovered in the 1930s.

- **From the 1980s**, dinosaur discoveries in almost every province of China have amazed scientists around the globe.

- **Some finds** in China have been fakes, such as part of a bird skeleton that was joined to a part-skeleton of a dinosaur along a natural-looking crack in the rock.

- **Some better-known Chinese finds** include *Mamenchisaurus*, *Psittacosaurus*, *Tuojiangosaurus* and *Avimimus*.

- **Remains of the prosauropod** *Lufengosaurus* were found in China's southern province of Yunnan, in 1941.

- **China's *Lufengosaurus*** lived during the Early Jurassic Period, and measured about 6–7 m in length.

- **Many recently found fossils** in China are of feathered dinosaurs such as *Caudipteryx*, *Sinosauropteryx* and *Microraptor*.

▼ Recent fossil finds in China are causing scientists to change many long-held ideas.

Australia

- **In the past 50 years**, some of the most exciting discoveries of dinosaur fossils have come from Australia.

- **Remains of *Muttaburrasaurus***, a large plant-eater, were found near Muttaburra, Queensland.

- ***Muttaburrasaurus*** was about 8 m long and similar in some ways to the well-known plant-eater *Iguanodon*.

- **Fossils of *Rhoetosaurus***, a giant plant-eater, were found in 1924 in southern Queensland.

- **The sauropod *Rhoetosaurus*** was about 15 m long and lived about 180–160 mya.

- **Near Winton, Queensland**, over 3300 footprints show where about 130 dinosaurs once passed by.

- **One of the major fossil sites** in Australia is Dinosaur Cove, on the coast near Melbourne, Victoria.

- **Fossil-rich rocks** at Dinosaur Cove are part of the Otway-Strzelecki mountain ranges, and are 120–110 million years old.

- **Remains found** at Dinosaur Cove include *Leaellynasaura*, a smaller version of the huge meat-eater *Allosaurus*, and the 3-m, 120-kg plant-eater *Atlascopcosaurus*.

▼ Many exciting fossils have been found in Australia over the past 50 years – most of these are found nowhere else in the world.

North America

- **Most dinosaur fossils** are from North America.

- **Many of these fossils** are from the West region, which includes the states of Montana, Wyoming, Utah, Colorado and Arizona and Alberta in Canada.

- **Several sites** in North America are national parks.

- **The US Dinosaur National Monument**, on the border of Utah and Colorado, was established in 1915.

- **The Cleveland-Lloyd Dinosaur Quarry** in Utah contains fossils of stegosaurs, ankylosaurs, sauropods and meat-eaters such as *Allosaurus*.

- **Along the Red Deer River** in Alberta, a large area containing thousands of fossils has been designated the Dinosaur Provincial Park.

- **Fossils found in Alberta** include *Albertosaurus*, *Euoplocephalus* and *Lambeosaurus*.

- **The Dinosaur Provincial Park** in Alberta is a United Nations World Heritage Site – an area of outstanding natural importance.

- **A huge, 20-m-long plant-eater** was named *Alamosaurus* from the Ojo Alamo rock formations, now known as Kirtland Shales, in New Mexico, USA.

▲ *This map shows some of the most important fossil sites of North America. Remains of some of the most famous dinosaurs have been found at these locations, including* Allosaurus, Tyrannosaurus, Diplodocus, Triceratops *and* Stegosaurus.

Dinosaur National Monument

- **Dinosaur National Monument** is a protected area in the southwest of America, spanning the border between the states of Colorado and Utah.

- **It was one of the first sites** in the world to be given special protection for having fossils, back in 1915. Today it covers more than 85,000 hectares.

- **The rocks** at Dinosaur National Monument were originally the banks and bed of a river, where animal bodies were washed during floods, and preserved.

- **The area contains** not only the fossil-rich Dinosaur Quarry, but also surrounding beautiful areas of the Uinta Mountains and the Yampa and Green Rivers.

- **Today's harsh climate** at the Dinosaur National Monument area means many rocks are bare and wear away, or erode, to reveal thousands of fossils.

- **Remains of more than 20 kinds** of dinosaurs and similar creatures have been found here, including the meat-eaters *Allosaurus* and *Ceratosaurus*.

- **There are also fossils** of the 'ABCD' plant-eating sauropods *Apatosaurus*, *Barosaurus*, *Camarasaurus* and *Diplodocus*, and plate-backed *Stegosaurus*.

- **Dinosaur National Monument** receives up to half a million visitors each year.

- **At Dinosaur Wall** in the Quarry visitor centre, people can see jumbled fossil bones and other remains sticking out of the rocks.

▼ *A field worker carefully excavates fossil bones on a sloping rock layer at Dinosaur National Monument.*

South America

● **Many of the most important** discoveries of dinosaur fossils in the last 30 years were made in South America.

● **Dinosaur fossils** have been found from north to south of the continent, in the countries of Brazil and Argentina.

● **Most fossils** have been found on the high grassland, scrub and semi-desert of southern Brazil and Argentina.

● **Some of the earliest dinosaurs**, such as *Herrerasaurus*, lived more than 225 mya in Argentina.

● **Some of the last dinosaurs**, such as the sauropods *Saltasaurus* and *Titanosaurus*, also lived in Argentina.

● **Fossils of the meat-eating predator** *Piatnitzkysaurus* come from Cerro Condo in southern Argentina.

● *Piatnitzkysaurus* **was similar** to the great predator *Allosaurus* of North America, but at 4–5 m long, it was less than half its size.

● *Piatnitzkysaurus* lived during the Middle–Late Jurassic Period, like many dinosaurs in Argentina.

● **Remains of about ten huge** *Patagosaurus* sauropods were found in the fossil-rich region of Chubut, Argentina, from 1977.

Boyacá
(Columbia)

El Breté (Argentina)
Cerro Rajada
(Argentina)
Santa Maria (Brazil)
Neuquen
(Argentina)
Ischigualasto
(Argentina)
Cerro Condor (Argentina)
Santa Cruz (Argentina)

▲ *Dinosaur fossils found in South America since the 1970s reveal unique kinds of meat-eaters, among the biggest predatory dinosaurs, some of the earliest members of the dinosaur group, and possibly the largest of all dinosaurs, Argentinosaurus.*

Antarctic dinosaurs

▼ Cryolophosaurus *fossils were found in the same region as those of sauropod dinosaurs, pterosaurs and therapsids (mammal-like reptiles) the size of rats.*

● **The huge continent of Antarctica** has not always been ice-covered at the South Pole.

● **Through parts of prehistory**, Antarctica was joined to Australia, and the climate was much warmer, allowing forests with trees and bushes to grow.

● **This happened** during the Early Jurassic Period, 201–174 mya, and again in the Early Cretaceous Period, 145–100 mya.

● **At this time**, insects, worms, reptiles such as dinosaurs and crocodiles and flying pterosaurs, mammals and many other creatures lived in Australia, and fossils of some have been found on Antarctica.

● **Finding fossils** on Antarctica is very difficult, with intense cold, bitter winds, blizzards, and rocks covered with ice and snow for most of the year.

● **The first dinosaur fossils** found on Antarctica were dug out in 1986 on James Ross Island, at the tip of the Antarctic Peninsula, south of South America.

● **The dinosaur**, of the ankylosaur or armoured dinosaur group, was named *Antarctopelta*, meaning 'Antarctic shield'.

● *Antarctopelta* **was about 4 m long**, weighed up to one tonne, and lived about 70 mya.

● **The first discovery** of a meat-eating dinosaur on Antarctica was *Cryolophosaurus*, in 1991.

● *Cryolophosaurus* **lived** during the Early Jurassic Period, some 190 mya. It was about 6 m long and weighed up to half a tonne.

● **The name** *Cryolophosaurus* means 'frozen crest lizard' because this dinosaur had a bony crest that rose up between its eyes and had a comb-like tip.

Index

Entries in **bold** refer to main entries; entries in *italics* refer to illustrations.